THE DEVIL AND THE CHILDREN OF GOD AT THE END OF THE WORLD

THE
DEVIL
AND THE
CHILDREN
OF GOD
AT THE
END OF THE
WORLD

MATTHEW DEIBLER

THE LAMP
ON THE STAND
PUBLISHING

THE DEVIL AND THE CHILDREN OF GOD AT THE END OF THE WORLD

ISBN 978-1-5445-1892-3 *Hardcover*
      978-1-5445-1891-6 *Paperback*
      978-1-5445-1890-9 *Ebook*

This book is dedicated to my Lord and Savior, Jesus Christ. You are the author of my life. I will always fight for the Truth, for the sake of my children and for all of the children of God.

CONTENTS

INTRODUCTION

GOD CHOSE ME

I AM NOT A PERFECT CHRISTIAN. IN NO WAY HAS MY life been a standard for righteousness. In fact, my story is littered with sin.

Throughout my life journey, I assumed many roles:

- Silent sufferer
- Tormented teen
- Escape artist
- Control freak
- Degenerate gambler
- Panic-ridden pawn of evil

All of these roles were completely out of alignment with the will of my Creator. That's because, for the first twenty-nine years of my time on this earth, I assumed the identity of a victim. I didn't know God, and I had zero understanding as to how the forces of evil were influencing my life. I blamed everything on circumstance. I enabled the devil. I lost my desire to live.

In the eyes of others, I was perhaps one of the least likely individuals anyone would anticipate to see called into a critical role for God's children and His Kingdom. For most of my life, I would have agreed with them wholeheartedly. Thankfully, however, it didn't matter what I thought about myself or what anyone else thought about me. Because...

...where I saw weakness, God saw strength

...where I saw pain, God saw purpose

...where I saw failure, God saw redemption

...where I saw the end, God saw the beginning

You see, "God chose the foolish things of the world to shame the wise; God chose the weak things of the world to shame the strong. God chose the lowly things of this world and the despised things—and the things that are not—to nullify the things that are, so that no one may boast before him" (1 Corinthians 1:27–29).

GOD CHOSE ME

One in 300 million chosen for the perfect marriage with the egg of my mother in order to gain life in this world. That's absolutely mind-boggling. That's a miracle. That's God.

When I encounter people who are having a hard time maintaining faith in the Lord's ability to miraculously intervene and offer healing and transformation, I first attempt to help them recognize the absolutely miraculous nature of their own existence. I tell them that they've been given life with great intention. I remind them that God chose them.

I'm here to help you understand that God chose you, too.

Even if you find yourself in a season of life where it's been difficult for you to see God...

Even if you've grown weary...

Even if you've been misled...

Even if you've lost hope...

No matter where you are in your spiritual journey, the fact of the matter is that you remain His perfect creation. You are a child of God. He retains the same divine calling for you that He ordained the moment that He formed you in your mother's womb.

Circumstances do not change that. A troubled past does not change that. No one can deny you God's everlasting love. Not even the devil himself.

But he will try. Oh, he will try. Satan is committed to distracting, deceiving, and dividing the children of God. He is the adversary of the Truth. He is very real. I know him well. Because I encountered him directly twice in a seven-year period in the wake of my rebirth in Christ as God's mission for my life began to come into focus.

Days after my final resistance of the devil in the summer of 2020, as I unpacked the depth of all the deceit that I had managed to escape in the strength of the Lord, I felt called to share my story. It was a command that I could not ignore. I could sense the urgency behind the nudge that I received from the Holy Spirit. I knew that my testimony needed to be spread among both believers and nonbelievers alike. God was calling me to reveal to His children the inner workings of the devil so that they, too, could escape the deception of the father of lies and navigate their way back home to the Truth before the return of our Lord and Savior Jesus Christ.

Speaking about the devil demands a level of boldness and bravery that only the Lord Himself can provide. I never anticipated that God would use my life in this manner. But He chose me. He delivered me from evil. I took His call to share my redemption story very seriously. I owe my life to Him. I am honored to glorify His Name.

Many signs are beginning to indicate that we are approaching the End Times prophesied in Scripture. I've had several dreams and visions that have appeared to confirm for me that this notion is true. That being said, only the Father knows the day and the hour. What I can tell you is that I feel the Holy Spirit guiding me now with a sense of urgency that I have never experienced at any other point in my life. That's why I do not take this mission lightly. We may not have much time. Eternity is at stake.

The children of God are under attack in the world today. These are children with missions of great purpose and influence for the Kingdom of God. The time remaining to fulfill the call of the Lord and seek salvation in advance of the return of Christ is evaporating quickly.

We are about to witness levels of deception that we have never seen before. The father of lies is going to pull out all of the stops to rob believers of their voice and the eternal salvation that they've been offered through the blood of Jesus Christ. If you are a child of God and you stand for all that is Faithful and True, you can expect that you will be targeted. In the event that the devil does seek you directly, you will need to be prepared to stand firm in the face of temptation so that you can identify the nature of the deception and resist in the Holy Spirit and the Word of God. Jesus has reminded us all to "be ready" as he guides us to prepare and watch with a sense of expectancy and urgency.

In the chapters that follow, I will share with you my testimony and God's victory over the devil in my own life.

From the time that I was a young boy, I was influenced by the forces of evil. This book will reveal to you how those influences introduced trauma into my life that resulted in the suppression of shame. Shame that cast me deep into the throes of mental illness, leading up to my nervous breakdown, which inspired my eventual rebirth in faith and my miraculous journey out of agoraphobic captivity.

As I outline the story of my healing and my newfound life mission, I'll speak about my first encounter with the devil who arrived to destroy God's will for my life, and I'll share the pain of the troubling season that followed as I fell back into the temptations of Satan. I'll address the spiritual longing that I experienced in the years after my rebellion and the prophetic word and vision that finally arrived in advance of a miracle that turned my Spirit life back on with a heightened sense of urgency as I awakened in preparation for my new calling in the Lord.

Then I'll describe the culmination of my battle with evil as I dive deep into the lessons that I learned in the midst of the greatest fight of my life. It occurred during my second direct encounter with Satan, who arrived in 2020 to finish the work that he began seven years earlier. I'll share with you the indicators that God presented to me through His Word to help me identify the nature of my deceiver as I journeyed for forty days and nights deep into the wilderness in advance of my last great temptation. I'll speak about the devil's underlying schemes and the three foundational temptations that he uses to entice and lead astray the children of God. Last but not least, I'll share with you guidance on how to resist the devil's advances so that when Jesus Christ returns in all His Glory, you too will be prepared to return home to Your Father in Heaven.

The complexities of the devil's handbook are many. But trust that the Father loves us deeply. Every hair on our heads was created in His perfect intention. He has a sincere interest in guiding us to eternity in His Kingdom. So fear not. Remember, you were chosen.

The victory is ours. We need only to claim it.

CHAPTER I

THE FATHER
OF LIES

ON THE DAY OF MY BIRTH, I BECAME A MARKED TARGET
of the evil one. I understand that's not a pleasant thought
to absorb. But it's true. The devil has a sincere interest in
children. He has a distinct appetite for disrupting our walk
with God and interfering with the divine plan that the Lord
has ordained for our lives. He knows that the best way to
reduce a man or woman of God is to influence them early
and often when they are children before they ever reach the
maturity to live the Word of God independently as adults.
For me, the courtship started while I was a young boy. I can
speculate about the conditions that led to my vulnerability,
but it's difficult to draw any definitive conclusions as to what
created the opening for evil to take root.

I was baptized in the Lutheran church. I attended Sunday

school and catechism class leading up to my first communion. By traditional religious standards, my parents were guiding me to follow the playbook of modern Christianity. But I never felt at home in our church. I'll be honest, I really didn't enjoy attending the services. They were very dry and mundane, and when I was little, I spent countless Sunday mornings arguing with my parents about going. I didn't have fun there. I wasn't motivated to grow my understanding of the Word or my faith within those doors. The atmosphere felt staged and insincere.

Beyond the disconnect that I felt with my religion, I also grew up in a home where there was quite a bit of strife. I love my parents, and I am grateful for everything that they have done for me. As a child, I never doubted their love for me as their son. I did, however, have many questions about their love for each other. That troubled me. To the outside world, we looked like a quintessential family because on the surface, we had it all together. The neutral observer wasn't able to see the arguments that I witnessed behind closed doors, arguments that led to unresolved tension and resentment that deeply influenced me. I often felt an extraordinary amount of anxiety and pressure in that environment: pressure to conceal our family's true identity and pressure to bridge the gap in my parents' marriage for fear that it may collapse at any moment. The uncertainty weighed heavily on me. There was a lot of negative energy in our home. I learned that later in life. Through my study of demonic influence, I have come to understand that strife in the home often can open a door to the intrusion of dark entities among children.

Then there was the worldly influence. Hollywood. Growing up, my mother followed a daytime soap opera called *Days of Our Lives*. In 1995, the show highlighted a demonic possession of one of its main characters, Marlena Evans. I believe the storyline covered a three-month period extending from May until July of that year. I was twelve years old and heading out of school for my summer break. Frequently, I caught pieces of those episodes while I was at home with my mom. They terrified me. I began to develop a sincere fear of the devil that had not been present in my life prior to that time. This then led to great anxiety. Anytime I walked into a dark room, I checked for red eyes in the corner. In the years since, I've often wondered, in my weakened state of vulnerability, had I unknowingly given the devil the upper hand in my spiritual development?

There were undoubtedly a number of factors contributing to my susceptibility to demonic influence. In any case, the devil's perfect gateway cocktail seemed to have been concocted by my early adolescence. That was the period of my life when I recall first encountering obsessive-compulsive thoughts. These thoughts were not my own. They were planted there. My brain churned on them and sought to deal with them in the fashion that it best understood, which was in the flesh.

As an adolescent, I had zero understanding of the deceptive

schemes of the devil. So I had no way of identifying his influence, and I certainly wasn't mature enough to handle spiritual warfare anyway. I believed that I held the responsibility for my intrusive negative thoughts, and that led to a lot of shame, guilt, and pressure. I was embarrassed, and I sought to hide the depth of my suffering so that I would not be judged. No one needed to know about my fear of getting a woman pregnant or my incessant hypochondria. They certainly didn't need to know about my apprehension regarding the depraved minds of child molesters, nor did they need to be given access to the racing images that dropped into my brain of people being hurt or dying.

Imagine having those types of things come to you without permission. Imagine accepting responsibility and praying for forgiveness for thoughts that you openly acknowledged were not welcome in your own mind.

The devil was force-feeding me lies, and I lacked the faith, knowledge, and strength to resist. I was essentially powerless to his influence. I knew nothing about the armor of God spoken of in Ephesians chapter 6. I had simply fallen on board a ship headed down a sea of destruction without any recognition of who was steering the vessel. Life continued on, but my innocence had been lost. I felt as though I had been robbed. I often wondered, why did things have to be so difficult? Why did I need to fight this secret battle while my friends were enjoying their teenage years without worry?

Why was there so much pressure to simply persevere in my thoughts day to day? What had I done wrong?

The reality is, I hadn't done anything wrong. I was simply a child of God born with a mission to serve in His name. The devil had me in his sights from a very early age. He was seeking to disrupt my calling before it was ever able to fully reveal itself to me. Although his tactics were extraordinarily crafty, his broader scheme was one that has been repeatedly used for thousands of years among many of his targets. The primary objective? Distract the children of God from realizing the purposeful missions that the Lord has called them to fulfill.

You see, the devil cannot by his own strength steal from you the destiny that God has ordained for you. But he can tempt you with his lies and poke and prod at you with influences beyond your control to try and steer your eyes away from the Truth. When targeting God's children, he often works in a manner that seeks to diminish an individual's identity, generally through trauma that results in shame, guilt, fear, or perhaps a combination of all three. These emotions lead to pressure—pressure to conceal the trauma itself along with the ongoing pain and torment that has become present as a result.

The pressure to conceal then overwhelms that person, leading to things such as anxiety, depression, and rage. In such states of oppression, chaos floods the mind. Thoughts race, and fear runs rampant. Life becomes more about survival than purpose. It becomes hard to envision a destiny beyond a life filled with pain.

This is exactly what the devil desires. Where there is chaos, there is very little clarity. When we are committed to concealing, there is absolutely no space for revealing. So God's plan remains hidden from our eyes, ensuring that the mission that He has intended for our lives never has the opportunity to get off the ground. The evil one secures the victory, at least temporarily. For the only way that the devil can hurt God is by leading His children astray.

In this state of confusion and chaos is where many people find themselves feeling lost and hopeless. It's a state that I lived in for nearly two decades. I wandered aimlessly from adversity to adversity and heartache to heartache, completely unaware of the negative influences of the spiritual realm in my life. I didn't know God, and I certainly wasn't seeking Him. That vulnerability made work easy for the devil because I was operating without any defense. Once the evil one had established a firm influence in my thought life and my foundational shame had taken root, there was very little more that he needed to do. My coping mechanisms and anxiety then continued to open the door to cycles of trauma that kept me treading water for many years to follow. And God's mission went unnoticed in my life, just as the devil intended.

CHAPTER 2

BEATING THE AIR

RECENTLY, I WAS ASKED BY A MENTOR OF MINE TO reflect on my childhood and share what I believed to be one of my greatest natural strengths. As I paused to think, I drifted back to my early involvement in athletics. I always loved to compete, and I really wanted to be the best at everything that I did. Thankfully, I had some God-given talent that allowed me to excel at nearly every sport I tried. That was very fulfilling to me. I felt confident and strong when I was competing athletically.

Although my talent was God-given, my work ethic and tenacity on the playing field was learned. My father was a former Division 1 college athlete. My appetite for competition was fueled by his passion and teaching, something that I embraced with open arms. The connection that my father and I shared through sports allowed me to build a very deep connection with him. He was an outstanding coach and support. He taught me how to overcome adversity by using many of the principles that he himself had applied as an athlete and a businessman.

The mindset and work ethic that I learned from my father was well intentioned. As I began battling my own adversities in life, I leaned more and more heavily on his teachings. Those strategies were very useful in the sense that they helped me to endure. They taught me perseverance. On the athletic field, in the classroom, and in all other facets of life, I understood the value of grit. I took pride in getting back up to play another down. I found myself repeatedly trudging forward "in spite of" to the point that I grew confident in my own independent ability to overcome anything that I faced. And it worked, to a point.

It worked until the battles grew bigger than my flesh. I began to realize that in my own strength, I was no match for my opposition. On the football field, I could overcome a third and long with my legs or my arm, but I could not dispel my obsessive mind or the anxiety that interfered with my ability to enjoy the freedom of the game that I once loved. I came to understand that at the core of every major adversity I faced in life was something far bigger than me. I was fighting my battle on the wrong playing field. My blueprint for success was useless. I could not win a war of the spirit realm in the flesh. But I had no other idea how to fight back. I didn't know God, and I didn't understand the devil's schemes. So I wandered aimlessly, beating at the air around my invisible enemy while continuing to lose ground daily.

In 2001, I graduated high school and moved nearly 3,000 miles across the country to pursue a long-established college football dream that was quickly losing its luster at a small school in Southern California. By summer workouts, the lies of the devil were beginning to once again overwhelm my mind. My tormenting thoughts were rooted in perfectionism. I punished myself with negative self-talk at every misstep. In the midst of the self-directed criticism, I began to actually resent football. It wasn't fun anymore. The devil had stolen the purity of it from me. I was tired of the abuse. So I quit. But I remained in school in California.

On a summer night one year later, I made a careless decision that changed my life dramatically. A friend of mine from my hometown in Pennsylvania had flown into LA for a visit, and we decided to smoke a little marijuana to let loose. I didn't know it at the time that we made the purchase, but the weed that we had acquired was laced with angel dust (or PCP). I was not at all prepared for the high that I was about to experience. My reaction was pure paranoia. It was quite possibly the worst night of my life. It opened a door to future torment that I would not be able to close for a long, long time.

In the days, weeks, and months that followed, I began experiencing intense anxiety and panic attacks. My appetite for a calming escape from reality had landed me directly into the hands of the devil. I had no understanding of what I was dealing with, and that alone was truly terrifying. My father in Pennsylvania became my sounding board. I would often call and speak to him for hours, many times late into the night as I tried to wrap my head around what was happening and find direction for a pathway forward. He'd stay awake just to ensure that I was okay. He truly sustained me and literally saved my life.

By the end of the fall semester, things were so bad that I had no choice but to move back east. Thankfully after about six months at home, the anxiety dissipated to the point that I felt comfortable leaving the nest once again. I transferred into the University of North Carolina, enrolling as a junior for the fall 2003 semester. I graduated from Chapel Hill in 2005, and soon after, I began a sales career in Philadelphia before moving out of the city and closer to the area where I grew up a year or so later.

As the years passed by, I continued to be plagued by the lies of the devil, and I spent many seasons in and out of the grips of mental illness. I still had no relationship with my Father in Heaven whatsoever. I was continuing to rely on my own strength and wisdom to sustain me. The pressure to persevere and conceal only continued to mount as the reality of my adult responsibilities began setting in. I felt overwhelmed. I needed an outlet to cope.

At the age of twenty-two, I made the regretful choice to finance a single large purchase that I could not afford with my current income on a credit card, creating a debt hole that powerfully triggered my obsessive mind. For years, I had been vulnerable and in need of an outlet for my racing thoughts, and this event simply accelerated my desperation.

I felt led to seek any means necessary to silence the misery of carrying the burden of anxiety attached to my debt. My solution was to gamble, a vice that deeply exacerbated my problem. The financial hole grew larger and larger, and I became enslaved to it. I became addicted to my fix, which served as a deposit on the extension of my captivity. Even when I hated the casino, I ran to it as false hope because it helped me silence the chaos in my head, if only momentarily.

The devil had me cornered. I had unknowingly given him permission to establish his ongoing influence in my thought life, and that allowed him to run significant interference in and among everything that I held near and dear to my heart. He sucked the life out of my dreams. He robbed me of my joy. In my desperation and desire to escape the pain, I found myself led to coping mechanisms that only deepened my shame. I was in a pit of darkness from which it seemed there may not be an escape. I couldn't even begin to envision a life that wasn't simply about survival. The devil was systematically breaking me down and destroying my hope. Once he was finished, he would then seek to destroy me.

CHAPTER 3

LED TO
CAPTIVITY

BY EARLY 2011, MY LIFE WAS REACHING A BREAKING
point. I was nearing the end of a toxic relationship, and I
could feel the anxiety from months of accumulated stress
pulsating beneath my skin. In early February, I suffered what
I believed to be a nervous breakdown. One week later, the
relationship ended, and my quality of life fell to a depth that
I had never experienced before.

Initially, things felt a bit like 2002, when I first encountered
anxiety and panic while I was living in California. But the
symptoms then quickly intensified beyond anything I had
ever known. My anxiety became persistent throughout the
daytime hours, and panic attacks became a frequent occurrence in the evenings as I attempted to rest.

Within a few months, I became agoraphobic, meaning that I became captive to my comfort zone. I was terrified to leave my apartment for fear that I would experience another nervous breakdown while out in public. The anxiety beyond the threshold of my front door grew so intense that I struggled to complete even the simplest of tasks such as taking out the trash or checking my mail. There were times when two weeks would pass before I left my apartment complex. I only got in my car when I had no other choice left to survive.

My agoraphobia was very clearly a reflection of my soul's captivity to the evil one. I was in deep, and the walls were closing in on me. The devil had robbed me of my appetite for life. In relationships, I simply moved from one heartache to the next, partly because I chose my partners for the wrong reasons, and also because I too brought a lot of baggage that undoubtedly weighed heavily on those whom I grew close to. Under the influence of Satan, I had become a slave to my vices, and I remained buried under a mountain of debt I felt like I would never escape. Every time I attempted to break the cycle, fear and doubt overwhelmed me as it coerced me back into the misery of my comfort. That comfort was stifling. I hated it, but I couldn't see another way out. So I fell into the captivity of solitude. At that point, the devil had me right where he wanted me—alone with my thoughts. Or perhaps better stated, alone with the thoughts that he was planting in me.

In the midst of my battle with agoraphobia, I again turned

to my gambling addiction as the escape for my chaotic mind. One weekend in July of 2011, I placed a bet on a women's soccer match out of sheer desperation. I knew nothing about the sport, let alone the teams involved in the wager, but I needed something to occupy my thoughts for a few hours.

As the match progressed, I began to recognize that I was going to be on the wrong side of the bet, and I got really angry. Out of that anger, I made a shameful ethnic slur that was completely uncharacteristic of who I was as a person. I smacked the screen of my laptop, shattering it and rendering it useless. Now what was I going to do? My lifeline, my access to the online sportsbook and virtual casino was dead. How would I ever survive the chaos of my mind in solitude moving forward?

I had no choice but to go buy a new laptop, I thought. So I muscled up the courage to get dressed and head over to Best Buy. As I walked to the register with a new device in my hands, I was shaking. I felt as though I was either going to throw up or pass out if I didn't get out of there ASAP. But I reminded myself that there were only a few minutes standing between me and my "perceived" freedom, and I pushed through it.

Upon reaching the parking lot, God intervened. There was a man exiting the car next to mine, and when he got out, he charged up to me in disgust, looked me dead in the eyes, and said, "Do I look like an a** to you?" Not coincidentally, this man was of the same ethnicity of the women's soccer athlete that I had verbally slammed within the privacy of my apartment just hours earlier. He was literally repeating and reminding me of my coldhearted slur in a completely unprovoked manner for no apparent reason whatsoever. I told him no, and I tried my best to avoid any further confrontation as I got into my car. Then I felt God's conviction wash over me. What had I become?

When I returned home, I was overwhelmed with nausea. I really didn't even want the laptop anymore. I felt shameful and dirty. I cleaned out the funds that remained in my online gaming account, and I stepped into the shower. That's when God spoke to me. As the water washed over me, I found myself reflecting on all the traumatic events of my life (financial losses, broken relationships, etc.) and I asked myself, what was the consistent theme in each of the seasons that I had lived through? Clear as day, God told me, "You. You were always present. Always a willing participant."

It was time to stop placing the blame elsewhere. I needed to take responsibility. Own it and seek forgiveness.

That night, I vowed to give up my gambling habit, and I started a blog. The very next day, I began writing about my journey in mental health. I was seeking to make things right with God and to offer my apologies to those whom I had harmed along the way. I dug into my open wounds coura-geously in faith, trusting in His Will and finding healing along the way. I disposed of my shame and my desire to conceal, and I started to reveal the purpose in my pain as my story began to inspire others and serve the needs of the broader mental health community.

But even as I began to redirect my life down a healthier spiritual path, my anxiety, panic, and more specifically, my agoraphobia only intensified. That year, I missed Thanksgiv-ing with my family, and I'll never forget the emptiness I felt on that day when I looked into my fridge. The only thing I saw inside was a single piece of fruit. No restaurants were open. Not even the McDonald's drive-thru. I celebrated with the fruit and whatever was left in my pantry until late in the evening when one of my family members was kind enough to bring me some leftovers. It was a very sad time in my life.

Soon after, I reached my rock bottom. One night while I was sitting alone in my apartment in complete despair, I fell to the floor in my bedroom under the weight of countless years of pain and evil torment. I found myself at a cross-roads. The devil's desires were being fulfilled. My tank was on empty. I had nothing left and no real hunger remaining for life. I couldn't see a way out, and I wanted desperately for the pain to end. I was ready to die. That, of course, made the evil one quite happy. His intention had always been to lead me to the point where I would take my own life and sacrifice my calling and my legacy. That was the true desire of his torment. Now I had a decision to make.

Thankfully, suicide was not an option for me. God had taken special interest in me, and He had directly intervened in my life. There was no denying it. When I began sharing my story, I felt His presence, and I sensed that He was not yet done with me, no matter how painful things seemed to be. We were just getting reacquainted. I was beginning to read the Word and seek His wisdom through devotional studies. I really wanted to believe in His ability to turn things around in my life. So that night, I brought my prayers to my Father in Heaven. I begged Him to take hold of me.

"If it is my time, take my life now. If not, take my life and do with it what You will. I have exhausted all of my options. I cannot do it anymore on my own."

Moments later, an affirmation came to me in divine fashion: "Let go…trust…believe…faith."

I ran to my computer, typed up the words, and placed them on my refrigerator. In the months that followed, I began inching my way forward in faith, repeating that affirmation with every step. By March, I had run one hundred miles on the treadmill in my apartment complex, and I was beginning to stretch boldly beyond my comfort zone to regain my life.

A true miracle in healing was unfolding through the work of faith alone.

In the wake of my rebirth in Christ, my Father in Heaven was delivering a powerful blow to His adversary, the devil. He was welcoming the prodigal son back home, and I was ready to glorify His name in gratitude for all of the amazing work that He had done in my life, rescuing me from the pit of darkness and giving my life new purpose and meaning. As I continued writing about my journey in mental health, I felt moved to share my complete testimony. So I prepared a thirty-two-page manuscript proposal for my first book and aligned myself with a publisher who was eager to print my story. I believed there was no better way for me to step into my calling and honor my Father in Heaven. God had rescued me from captivity. I was eager to glorify His Name.

CHAPTER 4

BORN AGAIN

BECOMING A BORN-AGAIN CHRISTIAN WAS THE BEST decision I ever made. I loved the freedom I felt in it. I repented, and my sins were forgiven. The weight that I had been carrying for more than fifteen years was finally gone. I no longer felt trapped by the troubled conditioning that had been established through the influence of Satan and his legion of demons. I was breaking the cycle and allowing the Father to direct my steps forward according to His Will. The pressure had evaporated. For the first time in my life, I didn't feel the burden of taking on the world on my own. In the arms of the Father, I had no fears or limitations.

I started living my life in a completely different manner than ever before. Everything had meaning to me. Nothing was coincidental. If God placed something in my path, I would seek His wisdom to decipher its purpose. I felt the guidance of the Holy Spirit. I trusted it. In the presence of other believers, I felt the power of God. I could sense the nature of a person's heart without really even knowing a thing about them. That same type of sensitivity and awareness also applied to the environments where I found myself conducting my life. If the space was unhealthy for me, I would be convicted by a deep-rooted discomfort. In moments when I began heading in the wrong direction, I could feel God cautioning my heart.

It was really a beautiful way to live. I felt as though I had finally uncovered the magic of a life led by faith. For years, the devil had done his best to cloud my vision and hide my Father's Truth behind a flood of incessant lies. Satan desired to hold me captive to a life that was not of my choosing. He tormented me and led away from God. In my flesh, I accommodated him through sin. I broke my Father's heart. But every single day, the Lord continued to love me the same. Now here He was, welcoming me home through the blood of His Son, Jesus Christ, and revealing to me the complete majesty of my rebirth.

In my season of renewal, I spent a lot of time reflecting on the work that God was doing in my life. I needed a miracle, and He provided. There was no denying that. I felt extremely grateful for His intervention. I recalled the life that I had left behind, and I thought, how did I ever allow things to get so dark? How could I have ever lived like that? In understanding the true essence of my soul through Christ, I was able to finally recognize how misaligned my steps had been for the vast majority of my days on this earth. I thought to myself, there's no way I'll ever go back.

I had stilled a chaotic mind and silenced the lies of the devil. I had regained my sanity and, more importantly, my soul. I had birthed a brand-new calling in the faith. I had found purpose in my pain. Purified by the blood of Jesus, I was made a brand-new creation. I was on the launch pad preparing for a mission beyond anything I could have ever envisioned in my natural mind. All that I had to do was trust the Father and continue to step forward in faith.

It sounded simple. I knew that it was the correct path because the Spirit was guiding me with sincere conviction in the will of the Father. But my flesh continued to war against the resurrection that I was experiencing. I was a marked target, and the devil fully understood my weaknesses, having exploited them countless times in years prior.

As I began preparing to proclaim God's glory and do His work, Satan took a very committed interest in my life once again. This time, however, it felt like he wasn't planning to simply send his legion of demons to torment me and disrupt my thought life. It was now personal. He was going to pay me a visit directly before I made any moves that would further disrupt his influence over God's children.

CHAPTER 5

LOST IN
TEMPTATION

FOR MY ENTIRE LIFE LEADING UP TO MY REBIRTH, I had worked to control the outcomes. I was a stubborn-minded perfectionist. I had developed a pattern of self-seeking rebellion in my life as I fell under the influence of Satan. It never mattered to me whether my path was aligned with God's. When I made a declaration to achieve something, I was going to make it happen one way or another, period. Any adversity I faced in opposition to my will, I would confront with a steadfast determination and work ethic. That was how I was taught. Persevere and grind for what you want. This is the world's defined pathway to success. But of course, we know that the world is at odds with our Father in Heaven. So it should be no surprise that I too found myself in resistance to Him and His call for my life. This is exactly what the adversary intended.

My past had been focused on attaining the things that gratified the desires of my flesh. I had relied completely on my own strength to achieve any goals that I had established for my life. Twenty-nine years had been all about me, but that wasn't going to be the way forward. Remember that I fell to my knees and begged the Father to either take my life or take me and do with me according to His will. So I could no longer live for me. I could only live for Him in the Spirit.

The beauty in living for the Spirit was that it required no analysis, no worry, and no pressure. I didn't need to figure out a thing. The only thing asked of me was that I remain deep in faith and allow for God's will to guide my steps. That meant taking action when I was called. Oftentimes, that required an uncommon boldness that was at odds with my earthly desires.

The Spirit called me to step out of my known comforts and into the vulnerability of a life led in true faith. In a sense, my Father was replicating the path that He had led me down to break the captivity of my agoraphobia. One step at a time: let go…trust…believe…faith. "You don't have to see the whole staircase," as Dr. Martin Luther King famously stated. "Just take the first step in faith."

God delivered me boldly. He led me out of the pit of despair by calling me to very publicly seek forgiveness and take ownership of my life. He encouraged me to develop a blog that transformed my journey in mental health and inspired me to rebuild my lost relationship with Him. In sharing my story, I felt a broader calling unfold. Armed with the mindset of a servant for His Kingdom, I would utilize my experiences to provide hope to others who were suffering and act as a catalyst for healing and spiritual renewal. It was clear I needed to have my story published. Where that would lead me, I had no idea—one step at a time. Get the book done. Trust God to reveal the path beyond that point.

This was a critical time in my life. I was embracing the Spirit's presence, and in a sense, I was getting ready to begin my own ministry. Thinking back to Scripture, I am reminded of Jesus's visit to the wilderness following His baptism in the Jordan River. Prior to beginning His powerful ministry, Christ felt Himself being led by the Spirit to the desert where He would fast for forty days and nights in solitude in order to draw closer in relationship with His Father. Then He would confront the devil.

That period of fasting must have been extraordinarily valuable to Jesus. By the time the devil approached Him, He was undoubtedly depleted and greatly weakened physically by the effects of starvation. Yet He stood with incredible might in His resistance to the temptations of the evil one, stronger on day forty than He would have been on day one. Not by the flesh, or His own strength, but by the Spirit and the Word of God, His Father in Heaven.

Jesus recognized that in order to do the Father's work and fulfill the mission He was called to serve, He needed to remain in Him and in the Spirit at all times. He needed to consume His Father's teachings and earnestly seek His guidance in every step to ensure He was never misled by the flesh or left vulnerable to the deceptive schemes of Satan. Remember, Jesus lived His victory by these words: "Yet not my will, but yours be done." He understood the pain and the torment of the flesh, but He chose to follow God's Will anyway. Jesus is the gold standard of childlike obedience in faith.

I wish that I could tell you that I followed His lead in my own mission, but I didn't. I was disobedient to God's calling. My self-centered desires led me astray once again, and the focus shifted back to me. Make more money. Take more trips. Buy more things. Build a comfortable life. God was directing me somewhere that felt ambiguous, and my flesh didn't appreciate having to wait to be blessed. So it sought to create its own blessings. It rebelled in the desire to define its future solely on its own.

It was during this period, in the spring of 2013, when I met the devil for the very first time. I found him in the financial markets as I began dabbling in risky, high-volatility trading as a means for making fast money in the absence of my gambling habit. Nearly two years had passed since I had given up my vice for the sake of my renewal in Christ. But as I began to drift further away from the Truth and closer to the temptations of my flesh, those desires reemerged.

I didn't want to renege on the promise that I had made to God to not place another wager or head back to the casino, so I developed a crafty workaround in the stock market. I convinced myself that I wasn't gambling because of the apparent legitimacy of the markets and the time and research that I was devoting to my trades. But that's exactly what I was doing, and the stakes were now higher than ever before.

In my trading research, I sought out newly established companies with high growth potential that were undervalued in trending markets. I wanted to find those who were flying under the radar of the public eye because that's where I believed that I could achieve the greatest return. So one day, I located a company that looked appealing to me, and in applying my standard due diligence, I made a phone call. On the other end of the line was my well-disguised adversary, salivating at my arrival and eager to lure me into his deception.

I explained to him my interest in the company, and we talked business for the better part of that afternoon. I was impressed, and I was deeply moved by his positive energy. He was very enthusiastic about the business's growth potential, and he shared with me that he, too, was a man of powerful faith. He believed that God had His hands on the business. That touched me. I wanted to believe that I was led to this seemingly and potentially life-changing opportunity for the right reasons. I wanted to believe that the Lord was in it.

Following that call, I immediately made an investment in the business, and my interest in the opportunity quickly began consuming me. Two weeks later, I advised my publisher that I would be abandoning my book project. I made every excuse imaginable. Not enough time. Not enough money. No understanding as to how I would build a business from it. No focus to write. The fact of the matter was, my calling was no longer a priority. My spirit life had been placed on the back burner yet again. God's mission fell second in line to my own interests. In a sense, I was trying to be the god of my own life, very much like the fallen angel Lucifer who, interestingly enough, was right there to embrace me in my own fall from grace.

As if that decision alone was not enough, I went further. I wanted to have a greater influence in the company's growth efforts, so I got involved with the business by offering my time and services to its cause. It was at that point when I met my deceiver face-to-face.

I'll never forget the conviction that the Holy Spirit poured over me in that moment. I recognized immediately that I was in the presence of pure evil. His aura made my stomach turn. I wanted to run and never look back. But I fought the commands of Truth and decided to stay for the sake of another leader in the organization and for the business itself. For the next several months, I served the mission of an evil entity.

In that short time, I sacrificed nearly every ounce of my initial investment. I lost thousands of dollars in wages accrued that the business could not pay me. The shares that I accumulated as a result of my involvement were rendered essentially worthless. But none of those losses could compare to the sacrifice of the work toward my mission in faith. I had given up everything that mattered for absolutely nothing in return. I rebelled against God. I disregarded the call of the Holy Spirit. I realigned myself with the devil. I broke God's heart once again in spite of all that He had done for me, leading me to wonder, would our relationship ever be the same again?

CHAPTER 6

THIRSTING FOR REDEMPTION

BREAKING TIES WITH THE DEVIL WAS PAINFUL. I WAS angry. Really, really angry. I'm not sure that I ever felt so empty inside. I recognized what I had in my relationship with God, and in the wake of my agonizing fall, I was able to reflect on all that I had sacrificed for the temptations of my flesh. I felt as though I was starting over. It was as if I was back on the outside looking in. I yearned to reconnect with my Creator and the Holy Spirit in a powerful way once again. But for years, there was a bit of a silence from the Lord in my faith life.

That being said, not all hope was lost. I continued to read the Word of God. In different seasons, I created mission-inspired content to share with my network. I wanted desperately to reignite my relationship with my Father in Heaven. I longed for a life with meaning. I often questioned, *Can't we just please go back to the way things were before I messed it all up?* It was devastating to witness how fulfilling life could be and then lose it all. There was a better way, and I knew it. I chose to give it all away. That created a deep sorrow within my heart.

During the summer of 2014, I committed myself to writing fifty unique blog posts in fifty days to jump-start my fading spiritual battery. I had concluded that if I could get the ball rolling, God and the Holy Spirit would most certainly intervene and open a door for me to reconnect with my fallen mission. I finished the series on September 5, and less than two weeks later, I felt moved to reach out to my former publisher to see if they'd be open to entertaining a conversation about a new version of my initial manuscript. They expressed interest, and we agreed to speak.

In the meantime, the devil intervened once again. He sent chaos to my life with an out-of-state tenant eviction that I had to handle for a property I owned in Pennsylvania. I quickly became overwhelmed by my dealings with that situation and the corresponding conversations with my attorney. On October 1, 2014, two weeks after my initial outreach to the publisher, I placed the book project on hold once again. Another distraction. Another victory for the evil one.

Despite the devil's best efforts to lead me astray, God

remained patient in His love for me. In Proverbs chapter 3, it is written, "My son, do not despise the Lord's discipline, and do not resent his rebuke, because the Lord disciplines those he loves, as a father the son he delights in." No one else in my life could have ever offered the same level of patience that He granted me as I continued to fall back into temptation and sin. He was practicing what He preached. Our relationship was strained, but I knew that He had not thrown in the towel. He continued to minister to me with gentle nudges as I became more mature in my spiritual journey and learned to resist the desires of my flesh. I knew that someday, He would delight in me once again.

For the next couple of years, as I settled into the demands of a new work role and began establishing plans for a future with my soon-to-be wife, I grew a bit caught up in the busyness of life. On Valentine's Day in 2015, my wife and I got engaged in the garden next to our former church in Chapel Hill, North Carolina. One year later, we eloped on a beautiful South Florida beach at sunrise. To accommodate our work schedules, we postponed our honeymoon until the summer. On July 11, 2016, we departed for a week away in Punta Cana, Dominican Republic.

I was really looking forward to the break and the opportunity to slow things down a bit and seek some clarity. When we arrived, the setting (and the company) was so beautiful that it was easy to feel exceptionally close to God. I began praying earnestly. I started to feel that God was going to reveal something profound to me. I was tuned in, waiting for His signal to arrive. Then the Word came to me: "water."

"Water." Okay, God, but what do you mean by that? I reflected on it all week long without any firm conclusion. The thing that really touched me was that in the years following my nervous breakdown and my season of agoraphobia, I had become extraordinarily sensitive to dehydration. Water was a critical element in my life that I needed to constantly keep in focus. I had to monitor my intake to ensure I remained hydrated and in a healthy place physically. When I became depleted, my psychological and emotional well-being suffered as well. Some days, it felt as though I could never drink enough. So I thought perhaps His message was a reminder or a warning with regard to my consumption. It seemed to me to be the most relevant connection.

Two months later, on September 11, 2016, I was traveling for business, and I had recently drifted off to sleep at a Marriott Hotel in Bethesda, Maryland. I was abruptly awakened by a vision that appeared to me in the mirror on the wall near the foot of the bed. At 11:45 p.m., I frantically reached for my iPhone on the nightstand, opened up a new note, and began documenting my experience.

An hour earlier, I was deep in conversation with God, and I had asked Jesus to speak to me because I was dealing with some very unsettling anxiety. I requested that He offer me a sign so I could better understand the reason that I was being overcome by such feelings. This was the second time in a couple of weeks that I had experienced a rush of anxiety without an identifiable root cause.

In the note I questioned, "Was He alerting me? Calling me to attention? Preparing me for something BIG?"

In the midst of my prayerful conversation with the Lord, I had somehow dozed off. When I awakened, the vision appeared.

Here's how I described the event.

"When I opened my eyes across the room in the mirror, I saw a white horse coming toward me. Then shortly after, Christ's face appeared in place of the white horse. It was drifting toward me. I knew it was Him. I felt His presence. I shook and was overcome with a sense of security. The anxious feeling within me left."

At the time, I had no understanding of the Book of Revelation. I had never spent any time studying it. But following the vision, I couldn't help but wonder if there was a connection between a white horse and Jesus Christ. So I immediately did a quick Google search on my phone, and what I found gave me goose bumps.

In Revelation 19:11–16, John shares his vision for Jesus's second coming at the End Times:

> I saw heaven standing open and there before me was a white horse, whose rider is called Faithful and True. With justice he judges and wages war. His eyes are like blazing fire, and on his head are many crowns. He has a name written on him that no one knows but he himself. He is dressed in a robe dipped in blood, and his name is the Word of God. The armies of heaven were following him, riding on white horses and dressed in fine linen, white and clean. Coming out of his mouth is a sharp sword with which to strike down the nations. He will rule them with an iron scepter. He treads the winepress of the fury of the wrath of God Almighty. On his robe and on his thigh he has this name written: KING OF KINGS AND LORD OF LORDS.

Wow. I had so many questions.

Did God provide me with this vision to alert me to prepare for the period of tribulation in advance of the End Times? Was He leading me to the Book of Revelation so I could ready myself for the devil's grand deception that had been prophesied to mislead many believers in the final days? Did He share with me the white horse as a vision of security and salvation to hold near to my heart in the season of chaos that would soon begin to reveal itself to the world?

In the span of two months, I had received a prophetic Word

followed by a prophetic vision. I really wasn't quite sure how to tie the two together, but I sensed there was very likely a connection that God would reveal to me in due time. One thing was clear: there was a new sense of urgency beginning to unfold with regard to my faith life. Awaken and prepare. Focus on consuming the "water." Seek Christ for security and peace in moments of anxiety and during the periods of uncertainty that will unfold in the near future. For the end may be closer than we ever knew before.

Suddenly, the waiting began to make more sense. In the years following my rebellion, I was receiving the loving discipline of my Father in Heaven. He cared for me enough to shape and mold me into the best version of myself as He prepared me for a calling that surpassed anything I had previously envisioned, even in years prior when I had believed I was truly clear following my rebirth in Christ. This was far more significant. It was going to require some advanced training. No crash course. No CliffsNotes. No watering it down. This mission would demand a serious commitment. He needed to know I was prepared to handle it and that I was serious about taking it on this time.

Would I break my cycle of regression, withstand the temptations of the evil one and go all-in on faith in childlike obedience to His will? Would I listen to the voice of the Holy Spirit and trust in God wholeheartedly in the midst of any worldly chaos that may ensue as the end of all things drew near?

CHAPTER 7

CHOOSING FAITH

FROM A VERY EARLY AGE, THE DEVIL USED HIS INFLU-
ence in my thought life to ensure that I was continuously
operating from a place of fear and lack. He did this by presenting unsettling thoughts to me that caused my mind to
panic and yearn for a fix, or at minimum, a means to conceal.
I, of course, did not welcome these thoughts, but I could
not determine their origin, so I blamed myself for their
existence. I silently carried the shame that I felt for holding
them, which in time completely overwhelmed me. It created
a pressure so great that I became fixated on controlling my
environment and influencing outcomes of my experiences.
Unknowingly, I was assuming the role of a god in my own
life, just as the evil one had intended.

Reflecting back on my adolescence, I remember that as my
body began to mature physically, I developed a paralyzing
fear of getting a woman pregnant. When the thought first

presented itself to me, it struck with such power and influence that I felt compelled to oblige. As anxiety began to repeatedly torment my brain, I adjusted my behaviors to accommodate the fear. I was ashamed of my paranoia, so I spoke of the fear to no one. I simply swallowed it whole and worked to manipulate my environment as best as I possibly could so that I could conceal my irrationality. This was the introduction of my obsessive-compulsive disorder.

My apprehension around getting a woman pregnant was rooted in ignorance first and foremost because I was still years away from becoming sexually active. I had this illogical concern that I could spread my seed in the same manner that we think of germs being transmitted through the air and on surfaces. If I touched my private area and it was unclean or I sat on a toilet seat, for example, I believed that I needed to be extraordinarily cautious. I was continually working to sanitize everything with which I came into contact, and I developed an unhealthy obsession with hand washing as a result of my condition.

Beyond my lack of understanding, what really haunted me was the what-if. "What if I do get a woman pregnant? How will I ever provide? I'm far too young. I don't have the resources to support a baby, and it will ruin my life. What will my parents and peers think of me?" I felt tremendous pressure to ensure that I never had to answer these questions. I could not handle that level of condemnation and shame. Certainly, I would not be prepared to take on the responsibility of a baby.

As I grew older, my paranoia dissipated slightly. That was largely due to education but also because I understood that if anything ever did happen unexpectedly in a moment of intimacy, as an adult, I now had the means to figure it out. Even as a married man in my thirties, however, I resisted the idea of children because I never felt as though I was quite ready. I wanted to have all of our finances in order—debts paid off, a home that we owned, a healthy income, money in savings, and so forth. I was focused on my ability to provide. I also recognized that we were getting older quickly, and it might take quite some time before I could make those things a reality. So at some point, I was just going to need to step out in faith.

Stepping out in faith was going to mean breaking ties to a crippling, anxiety-ridden obsession that I had held silently in shame for more than two decades. It was going to mean once again making a committed effort to break free from the captivity of the evil one. It was going to mean listening to the Holy Spirit and choosing faith over fear.

For many years, I had no idea why the devil chose to take such a sincere interest in discouraging my path to fatherhood. It seemed as if he knew that fatherhood would reveal something of great spiritual significance to me. Perhaps he wanted to interfere with God's plans for my future children by destroying my legacy before it ever had the opportunity to manifest itself. No matter the intention, I sensed that he was deeply invested in disrupting this area of my life. Perhaps that's why he had made such a bold effort to lead me into captivity and destroy me before I even had the opportunity to meet my wife.

Thankfully, I made it through the fire of my captivity and my first encounter with Satan. By 2016, my focus was back on aligning my will with God's. As I reflected on the timing and meaning behind the vision that I had recently experienced of the white horse and Jesus, I recognized the sense of urgency behind a willing obedience. So I made an effort to set my fears of fatherhood aside and let go and lean on God to figure things out. Just two months later, on November 11, 2016, my son was conceived.

Having a child was going to truly test my faith. Our finances were far from perfect. I was still carrying a debt burden. We did not own a home, and there was very little in our savings accounts. My income was stable, but I was getting ready to assume the role of sole provider. We certainly weren't getting ahead, and it didn't look like that would be something to anticipate anytime in the near term. It was an imperfect setup by conventional standards. But I figured it was EXACTLY the way God wanted it.

Fatherhood was going to demand that I lean more heavily on my Father's Will than on my own. In order to become a father, I needed to trust the Father. To dispose of my irrational fears, I needed to embrace a deeper relationship with my faith. To undo more than twenty years of old conditioning that began with the infiltration of one strategically timed lie, I had to reveal the source of my deceit. To disarm evil, I needed to arm myself with the Truth. This was the battle that I had been fighting unknowingly all along. Fatherhood was about to reveal the great depth of the love and grace of the one true Father to me. It was time for me to ground myself in Him and trust not in my own strength but rather in His unique ability to provide.

CHAPTER 8

MY MESSENGER

AT 6:00 A.M., JULY 16, 2017, I WAS LYING IN BED WHEN I heard my wife call to me from the master bathroom. As my eyes sought to adjust to the light peeking into the bedroom from the bathroom door, I heard her say, "We are going to have a baby today."

I jumped out of bed. "Today? Are you serious?" Our baby's due date was two and a half weeks away. Perhaps this was simply a false alarm.

My wife then confirmed that she had been having contractions since 2:30 a.m.

"Since 2:30?" I asked. "Why didn't you wake me?"

She told me that she wanted to wait and see how things progressed to ensure that it was, in fact, the real thing. A few hours later, she had arrived at her conclusion. It was go time. We should begin taking this seriously and get ready to make our way to the hospital.

The following day at 10:46 a.m., after more than thirty-two hours of labor, my son entered the world and took his first breath. I will never ever forget that moment. When he arrived, I felt as though I escaped my body temporarily. It was as if I was being transported to a different dimension altogether and I was floating in the room. The sensation was overwhelming. Meeting my son for the first time was like staring into the eyes of God.

Witnessing the miracle of life and seeing the purity of God's perfect creation was something my heart could not prepare for in advance. No childbirth course, no YouTube tutorial, and no word-of-mouth testimonials from friends and family were enough to ready me for the rush of butterflies that almost angelically lifted me off my feet in the room that morning. God's presence was undeniable. Rarely do we have the opportunity to visibly experience His perfect will, but in those very brief moments following the birth of a child, we are able to see with our own eyes life in its most perfect form—exactly as God intended it to be, free from any contamination of the outside world, straight from the heart of our Creator.

This experience was exactly what the devil had been working so hard to deny me for the previous twenty years of my life. On the other side of my most debilitating fear was the greatest miracle that I would ever encounter. The devil didn't want me to come face-to-face with the heart of my Creator. Because he knew that once I did, I would understand the beauty of His Majesty and my eyes would never turn away from Him again. I would recognize the purity of His creation and the incredible value and purpose that He has carefully crafted and assigned to each of His children. As a witness to His amazing blessing through the eyes of my son, I would be given my own eyes to see that His same perfect intention was rooted within me as well. I would forever live with the understanding that the depth of His love far exceeded my own comprehension. I would never feel far from Him again.

We named our son Malachi. I made the suggestion to my wife over dinner one night because I really liked the sound of the name, and I knew it had a biblical connection. The meaning behind it was very special to us. Malachi means "My Messenger" or "Messenger of God." I sensed that our child was going to have a significant role among the Lord's children, so I really believed it was a perfect fit for our first-born son. My wife agreed.

Malachi serves as the last book in the Old Testament of the Bible. He was the final prophet to hear from God and share His Word before the arrival of John the Baptist. The world underwent 400 "Silent Years" following the writings of Malachi, who came at a time when people were really struggling to believe that God truly loved them. They were focused on the lack that they were experiencing. Instead of looking at their own sin, they allowed themselves to identify as victims of circumstance. Malachi urged the people to make changes, to own responsibility for their actions, and return to God and serve Him faithfully. Then he shared a final warning and message of hope:

> "Surely the day is coming; it will burn like a furnace. All the arrogant and every evildoer will be stubble, and the day that is coming will set them on fire," says the Lord Almighty. "Not a root or a branch will be left to them. But for you who revere my name, the sun of righteousness will rise with healing in its rays. And you will go out and frolic like well-fed calves. Then you will trample on the wicked; they will be ashes under the soles of your feet on the day when I act," says the Lord Almighty. (Malachi 4:1–2)

I absolutely loved this piece of Scripture. I could not deny the connection it shared with the prophetic dream that I had experienced two months to the day before Malachi's conception that was linked to the Book of Revelation and the second coming of Christ. The message from Malachi was about the End Times. It was serious, but it also carried a Word of peace for believers who turned their eyes and their hearts back to God.

Our firstborn son came into our lives in God's perfect timing for a very real reason. The name that was given to him was of no coincidence. We didn't choose it; the Spirit did. Like the former prophet, Malachi's arrival carried both a warning and a message of hope. Turn back to God and lean on Him and not on your own understanding in the midst of fear, uncertainty, and tribulation. And God will protect you from the wrath of evil, and you will rise triumphantly through redemptive healing at the time of His return.

July 17, 2017, seemed like a really special day to be born. What made it even more unique was that Malachi arrived seventeen days in advance of his due date, which was August 3. I couldn't help but wonder if there was perhaps another connection to Scripture. Then I found it in the Book of Revelation. Chapter 7, verse 17 reads, "*For the Lamb at the center of the throne will be their shepherd; he will lead them to springs of living water. And God will wipe away every tear from their eyes.*" Chills came over my body. There it was. "Water." The Word that I had received on the beach just two months prior to my vision of the white horse and Jesus Christ. That was it. My son's birth had tied the prophecies together. "Water" was the key. Not just any water but "living" water.

What is "living water"? Living water is the Holy Spirit. This is confirmed in the Gospel of John where Jesus states, "*If anyone thirsts, let him come to me and drink. Whoever believes in me, as the Scripture has said, 'Out of his heart will flow rivers of living water.'"* Then John goes on to say, *"Now this he said about the Spirit, whom those who believed in him were to receive, for as yet the Spirit had not been given, because Jesus was not yet glorified."*

We know that the Holy Spirit first descended upon the disciples on the day of Pentecost as Jesus promised prior to his crucifixion when He said, *"But the Advocate, the Holy Spirit, whom the Father will send in my name, will teach you all things and will remind you of everything I have said to you. Peace I leave with you; my peace I give you. I do not give to you as the world gives. Do not let your hearts be troubled and do not be afraid."*

God provides us with the Holy Spirit to help us navigate the uncertainties of life, and He allows us to maintain peace in a world that is growing more deeply at odds with Him each and every day. Notice that I said, "God provides." You'll recall from the previous chapter that my obsessive anxiety related to fatherhood was rooted in a fear surrounding my inability to provide. It was only when I let go and trusted the provision of God alone that my miracle, my precious son, Malachi, was conceived.

When Malachi came into this world, he carried a very distinct message for his father. *Understand what God can do. Trust His will. Embrace your purpose. Turn to Him to provide all things. As everything of this fallen world begins to falter,*

God's living water will sustain you, Dad. It will sustain us. It will be the hope and redemption for our family. Lead us in the Truth with the Holy Spirit as your guide. The time is now. It's never been more critical.

The children of God are living in a world that is broken. It's a world where the sinful nature of humanity has been magnified over thousands and thousands of years since Adam and Eve first rebelled against God in the Garden of Eden. The fallen angel, Lucifer, who became God's "adversary" or the evil one that we know today as Satan, was the serpent advocating for the sampling of the forbidden fruit from the Tree of Knowledge of Good and Evil. This curious sampling, of course, became the opening sin of humanity. But sin originated with Lucifer in the spiritual world before it ever existed here in the natural. That's the reason why Lucifer was cast out of heaven for eternity. That's why it's within this earthly realm that the devil has chosen to build his kingdom by deceiving the children of God and concealing His divine will for our lives.

Sin is difficult to escape in a world where morality has grown increasingly deficient. How do we even define purity in an environment where everything seems to be tainted with a touch of evil, self-seeking influence? We look to the innocent. God's perfectly untouched creation. We look to children. Because Jesus tells us to "let the little children come to me, and do not hinder them, for the kingdom of God belongs to such as these." He goes on to say, "Truly I tell you, anyone who will not receive the kingdom of God, like a little child will never enter it" (Luke 18:16–17).

Being a father is an amazing responsibility. The measure of care required as a shepherd of God's flock extends far beyond the basic carnal needs of any living being. As parents, we are called to embrace a spiritual relationship with our Creator that will allow us to guide our children in the way of the Truth. We must remember that the deck is stacked against them from the very moment they are born. They arrive into our lives as pure empty vessels of God. When they gain exposure to the world around them, they begin filling that vessel with the knowledge, influences, and biases that they are assigned. They start to build a foundation that will greatly define the nature of the beliefs that they will affirm and the personality that they will embody later on in life. The early inputs matter. So does their understanding of God.

The best way that we can lead our children in the Truth when they are young is by living it ourselves. We must love like God and allow our actions to be guided by the principles that Jesus taught His followers during His short time on this earth. The only way we can do that is by consuming the "living water" of the Holy Spirit, allowing it to direct every step that we take. This is where we often fall short, because we are the reflection of generations of flesh guided, sinful lifestyles that have fallen in opposition to God's Will.

The sins of humanity have been magnified from one generation to the next over thousands and thousands of years. Because of this, we can easily find ourselves lost within a heavy accumulation of wickedness where it can be extraordinarily difficult to decipher the voice of the Holy Spirit.

In order to prepare the legacy that we desire for our children, we must first earnestly seek our Father in Heaven in childlike obedience. We must yearn to hear the voice of the Holy Spirit. We must ground our words and our actions in the love of God and turn away from all evil. We must disregard the sinful path that the generations before us have chosen and offer our lives in reverent submission to His Will. We must purify ourselves and be born again in Christ, disengaging from any worldly conditioning that was previously rooted in us. We must seek God's Kingdom as a child, in the pure manner that He intended us to find Him on the day that we were born. To guide our children in God's Truth, we must lead them from a position of childlike faith and reliance on our own Father and the living water that He has provided us. We must confront and dispose of any ounce of evil that is in opposition to Him, including the devil himself.

CHAPTER 9

LEGACY VERSUS LUCIFER

WHEN MY SON WAS STILL IN HIS INFANCY, I QUICKLY began to recognize the critical nature of my role in his life as his father. Providing was always front of mind. But in getting to know my baby, in witnessing his mannerisms and understanding his sensitivities, I came to understand that I would need to reach him in ways that would extend far beyond his basic human needs. There would most certainly be a unique spiritual element required from me as well. I would need to trust God and His living water to reveal to me how to share that with him in due time.

It was clear to me that Malachi was quite the special baby. He was very specific in how he desired to receive soothing and comfort. What worked for a million other newborns was rarely the solution for my son. He yearned for something greater, something more specific. That resonated with me. Because through him, I could recall a similar unmet longing within myself, one that was established at a time when I, too, was very young. I sensed that Malachi may follow a similar path to my own. I wanted to effectively prepare him for the journey that was ahead of him in his life.

My focus began to shift away from my own desires and onto my son. I could feel the conviction of the Lord revealing to me that Malachi was destined to fulfill an extraordinary role in God's Kingdom. How could I ensure that he would be ready to accept the calling that God was going to place in his heart? What steps did I need to take as his father to begin outlining a blueprint for navigating the adversities of life that would undoubtedly come upon him as he grew older? How could I lead in such a way that would ensure that he was never led astray by evil?

The answer was clear. I needed to prepare my story for him. I felt moved to leave a legacy for my son to build upon. I knew that he was going to do far greater works than me. So it was critical that I provide the proper foundation from which he could embark on his own divine mission. As his father, it was my job to follow the example of Jesus Christ, who once said to His disciples, *"Very truly I tell you, whoever believes in me will do the works I have been doing, and they will do even greater things than these, because I am going to the Father"* (John 14:12).

To lead like Jesus, I had to empower the Holy Spirit within me. No more running to temptations. No more hiding from the Truth. No more distractions. No more lukewarm faith. It was time to reconnect with God and empower His voice within me once again. It was time to start living in a manner that would not only honor my own calling but my son's as well.

By early 2020, a ministry began developing within me. The global coronavirus pandemic was taking the main stage, and life in quarantine was becoming the new normal. People everywhere were beginning to face the harsh reality of social isolation and the vulnerabilities of anxiety, depression, addiction, and other related mental health conditions. Job losses were reaching levels that we hadn't seen since the Great Depression. Times were tough. The devil was clearly beginning to gain a foothold. That's when I began to feel the Holy Spirit nudge me. This was my time. This was God's time.

I understood social isolation intimately because I had survived agoraphobia. I recognized how very dark and all-consuming that environment could become when coupled with underlying mental illness and spiritual vulnerability. So I started reflecting on the experiences of my past, and I began sharing my story with bold transparency to inspire and guide those who were beginning to encounter the fight of their lives. The work became very rewarding. But I sensed there was more.

In sharing my own redemptive journey in mental health, I could not ignore the true victor. Faith is what had saved me. My mental health journey led to my rebirth in Christ. I began to heal when I allowed the Will of my Father to lead. He guided my steps forward, and I followed in childlike obedience. I needed a miracle, and He delivered. No drugs. No counseling. My redemption was through faith and faith alone. That's how He designed it for my life. My experiences were my initial training ground. In recognizing them as such, I found purpose in my pain.

God was the answer. I wasn't going to deny that. I didn't care if it was taboo to speak about Him in the public square. This was the Truth. I would be doing a disservice to Him and to the Holy Spirit if I didn't reveal it. So I started to weave God into my content around mental health because I understood fully that He was the key to redemption.

Then it happened. The moment I had been eagerly awaiting for years had arrived. Deep in my belly, I felt the conviction. The Father was preparing the way. The Spirit spoke to me. "Step into this full time. You cannot tiptoe around the Truth any longer. I need you to go all in."

I understood the call, but I fought it. I couldn't wrap my head around it. I kept questioning, "But how?" and "What about…?" The resistance made me feel physically ill. I was at the same wall that I had faced many years earlier following my rebirth as my book project came into focus and I began feeling overwhelmed. I wanted over the hump, but I didn't know how to make my vision a reality. Instead of trusting the Spirit and leaning into the Truth that had led me to the point of my breakthrough, I sought answers my own way, largely due to the persistent fear of my inability to provide for my family.

I knew in my heart that the only way I could truly provide as a father and as the leader of my family was by aligning myself with the Will of the Spirit. But I couldn't seem to let go of my own fear. So I sought some advice to propel me into the next phase of my life. I turned to social media to connect virtually with a spiritual mentor for guidance. Then, in walked the devil. Round two.

It was the perfect storm. I had been through years and years of training in preparation for my breakthrough in ministry. But the question remained—my will or His Will? I had one last obstacle to clear. The invisible enemy. How would I overcome the deceit of my spiritual adversary who had repeatedly led me away from the mission that my Father was calling me to serve? The answer was simple. By meeting him again. And denying him.

Like a serpent in the wilderness, God was going to make the evil one visible to me. Through the Word, the devil's deception was going to be revealed. The Spirit was growing strong within me once again. Now it was leading me to a purpose that extended far beyond the reach of my own life. This was about my legacy. It was about my son. It was time to overcome the flesh once and for all. It was time for spiritual warfare in the name of my own child and all of the children of God.

CHAPTER 10

THE BAD FRUIT

Watch out for false prophets. They come to you in sheep's cloth-
ing, but inwardly they are ferocious wolves. By their fruit you
will recognize them. Do people pick grapes from thornbushes,
or figs from thistles? Likewise, every good tree bears good fruit,
but a bad tree bears bad fruit. A good tree cannot bear bad fruit,
and a bad tree cannot bear good fruit. Every tree that does not
bear good fruit is cut down and thrown into the fire. Thus, by
their fruit you will recognize them. (Matthew 7:15–20)

I'VE ALWAYS WONDERED, WHEN JESUS EMBARKED ON
His journey to fast in the wilderness, did He recognize that
the Spirit was leading Him there in preparation to meet the
devil? What did He encounter in the forty days leading up
to the ultimate temptation that He faced? How did He speak
to His Father and grow in His faith in preparation for the
advance of the evil one?

Was the devil near to the Son of God throughout the forty days? Did he poke and prod at Jesus, waiting in the shadows until he believed that it was the opportune time to pounce? Did he send Jesus signals and mirages in order to deceive Him, setting the stage for an even grander temptation?

It's fascinating to try and imagine what those days of fasting, prayer, and waiting were like for the Son of God. Imagine if He had been carrying a journal to document the events. Think about the amazing mysteries He could have revealed about the schemes of the evil one as He readied Himself for battle in the strength of His Father.

I had long believed that the direct war with the devil was fought on a spiritual level that I would never fully be able to access. So I didn't anticipate that I would ever have the opportunity to uncover the true nature of that warfare in my own lifetime. Then I came to intimately know Satan myself. And many of the hidden mysteries of his deceptive schemes were revealed to me. The battle between good and evil was indeed very real. I was living it.

In the midst of my mental health and faith journeys, I had come to recognize some hidden strengths that the Father had revealed to me through His Holy Spirit. I call them my superpowers. My belief is that such uniquely fashioned God-given talents exist in all of us, and they are often found disguised in areas of our lives that we once perceived as flawed, perhaps when we were misaligned with the world, prior to a rebirth in faith. After all, God makes no mistakes in His creation. All is done with perfect intention.

Personally, I had arrived at the conclusion that my anxiety was simply my inability to effectively process my hyperawareness (or intuition). I recognize now that my hyperawareness is a tremendous gift when properly aligned with God. When I am able to create a calm heart and a still mind in faith, I can use my hyperawareness to my advantage. It doesn't present itself to me as anxiety at all. Instead, it shows up as my guiding light (the Holy Spirit) to help me navigate through positive and negative influences along with truth and deceit. Through my hyperawareness, I am able to hear my Father's voice and feel His presence. That allows me to direct my steps according to His Will.

But even with this superpower firmly established in both my heart and mind, I struggled mightily to reveal the devil's true identity. During my first encounter with the evil one back in 2013, I was far too consumed by temptation to allow the Spirit's voice to lead me. I heard the command of God, and I felt His nudge, but I tuned it out and pressed forward in defiant pursuit of my own will anyway. I suffered tremendous consequences for that decision. The Holy Spirit made every effort to illuminate the areas of my life that were turning dark, but in my desire to accommodate the appeals of my flesh, I refused to see. I became an enemy of the Truth.

Unknowingly, I aligned myself with the will of the devil, spiritually blind to the presence of my adversary, even as he stood right before me. In the years following that season, I often reflected on my experience, concluding that perhaps my deceiver was simply misled himself. Or maybe he really did have evil intent, but surely he wasn't the devil himself. He couldn't be, right?

I spent seven years of my life contemplating that notion. Seven years working my way back to God. Seven years dismantling temptations. Seven years extracting any of my remaining self-seeking vices. Seven years attempting to create the stillness of mind and heart that would allow me to once again hear the voice of the Holy Spirit.

At the midway point of that period, my son was born. In that experience, I felt the presence of the Lord in a way like never before in my life. The love and mercy of God flooded my being. The Father had blessed me in ways that I didn't deserve. He didn't give up on me when I turned my back on Him. Instead, He disciplined me and sharpened me for greater service to His Kingdom. Then He did the unthinkable. He gave me the greatest gift of my life. He made me a father. In doing so, He gave me a second chance. He gave me the eyes to witness His presence once again and to know that He was still near to me. That changed my life forever.

Being in the presence of my newborn son gave me tremendous faith. In his eyes, I saw God's promise. I saw my miracle. Malachi's arrival was confirmation that anything was possible through faith. I began believing and seeking the Holy Spirit in ways that I hadn't in years. Through my son, the Lord began to speak to me in preparation for all that was ahead.

Seven years and a miracle were leading me to my next fork in the road encounter with the evil one. Seven years was leading me to my own forty days and nights in the wilderness, literally. You heard it right. The devil's second pursuit of me followed the exact timeline of his temptation of Jesus Christ nearly two millennia prior. It was equally as ruthless. From the moment in May of 2020 that I was deceived into opening the door to his influence once again until the morning of my last great deception, exactly forty days and nights would pass.

In my first encounter, the devil's focus had been on breaking my will, or perhaps better stated, on destroying God's Will for my life. Shortly after the Holy Spirt first came upon me, he arrived to lead me into temptation and send me back to the captivity of lack that was consistent with the days prior to my rebirth in Christ.

When he returned in 2020, he came to fulfill part two of his exceptionally devious and extraordinarily tactful master plan. Just as I was advancing toward my divine mission in the power of the Holy Spirit, he made his presence known again. His goal in this meeting? To rob me of my soul for eternity and ensure that no child of God, including my own, would ever be able to hear the Truth spoken from my lips again.

The one thing that he failed to recognize in his approach, however, was the depth of God's love for me. Even as the devil's fire began to rage all around me, I remained under the care of the Lord. In the midst of his advance, the Holy Spirit began to reveal to me Scripture that had been placed in my heart at varying times over nearly a decade of study. Certain verses and parables would present themselves in my mind that I hadn't looked at closely in years. It was as if many of the seeds that had been planted in earlier seasons of my faith journey were finally beginning to bloom. They were rising in my soul and overflowing from my lips to dispel the fiery flames of the evil one.

In Matthew, chapter 7, Jesus warns of the false prophets. He tells us that we will recognize them by their fruit. Later, in Ephesians, chapter 6, Paul proclaims that the Word of God is the sword. As I began to diagnose the enemy, the Word in Matthew was my sword. In my mind, I heard it repeatedly. The Spirit was inspiring me to meditate on the notion of "bad fruit." I didn't immediately know what it was attempting to reveal, but I sensed that this Word was very important because it was present at all times, like a clock ticking in my brain. So I began to allow space for ongoing reflection. "Think about the fruit, Matthew. Anything that is evil cannot produce good fruit. What types of fruit does this deception bear?"

It took great patience, deep reflection in the Spirit, and continuous cross-checking with the Word through prayer to outwit, reveal, and resist the deception of the evil one. The devil is a highly intelligent being. That's what makes his work so truly powerful. He is extremely well versed in a very broad array of disciplines. It is difficult to challenge his knowledge, even in areas that you feel you understand well because he has a prompt and seemingly well-educated response to every question. He is adept at working his way out of any corner that you back him into because he is extraordinarily slick with his tongue. He is also quite charismatic. Mistaking his feigned kindness as sincerity only leads to peril. He exposes our weaknesses, and he uses them to his advantage to create loyalty. Make no mistake, if he seeks you, he desires you, and he is playing for keeps.

Identification is step number one in defeating Satan. It is extremely difficult to resist something that you cannot see. Most people who are being influenced by the dark forces of evil are only thinking in the natural. The adversity facing them doesn't appear on the surface to be spiritual in nature at all. But it is. That's a significant piece of the deceptive work of Satan. That's why it is absolutely critical that we first know our adversary.

Over the next ten chapters, I will expose the rotten fruit of the evil one that was revealed to me by the Spirit and through the Word as I worked to escape Satan's most grand deception and secure victory in the war for my soul during our second encounter in 2020. I will make clear to you influences that I encountered so that you too can dismantle the lies of the devil and stand firm in the Truth.

CHAPTER 11

THE BAD FRUIT

REINCARNATION

Now the serpent was more crafty than any of the wild animals
the Lord God had made. He said to the woman, "Did God
really say, 'You must not eat from any tree in the garden'?"

The woman said to the serpent, "We may eat fruit from the
trees in the garden, but God did say, 'You must not eat fruit
from the tree that is in the middle of the garden, and you must
not touch it, or you will die.'"

"You will not certainly die," the serpent said to the woman.
(Genesis 3:1–4)

SINCE HIS APPROACH OF ADAM AND EVE IN THE GARDEN
of Eden, the devil has been invested in spreading the lie of
reincarnation. Reincarnation is the belief that when we die,
our soul leaves our lifeless vessel and later returns to assume

another body. Within each lifetime, we grow and transition, and the things that we experience in future lifetimes are said to be the result of accrued karma from a prior season of our soul's journey. This type of belief system is highly evident in the Hindu religion.

Now, the devil did not openly approach me to draw me into Hinduism. He was wise enough to understand that a Hindu-rooted seduction would be an immediate disqualifier for any further faith-based dialogue with a Christian like myself. So he actually denounced it very early into our relationship with each other. Hinduism was the sole religion that he spoke outwardly against. I learned later the nature of those manipulative statements.

Reincarnation is a major no-no in the Christian faith. Beyond what the Scripture tells us, think for a second about what this belief would mean to our religion. First, it would presume that God somehow made a mistake in allowing for our souls to reside in living human vessels, because those vessels would leave our pure souls trapped within the prisons of our bodies. Further, reincarnation would reduce Christ's incarnation to a mere appearance, and it would mean that His death on the cross was simply an accident. Jesus would no longer be looked at as the only Son of God and the Lord and Savior. He would be diminished to an avatar of sorts, a term that the evil one himself used to describe his own version of Jesus to me.

When my deceiver initially presented the idea of reincarnation, I wasn't immediately receptive. In sharing his beliefs, he first described to me his own unique soul journey. He claimed to have crossed through many lifetimes over thousands of years in preparation for the season that we found ourselves in. He indicated that his soul once had a very dark element to it. There were heinous acts that he had committed against the most vulnerable in a previous lifetime. He was aware of them because he had accessed the memory of those events through transcendental meditation. His knowledge of the experiences had led him to believe that he was uniquely equipped to lead those presently found on a similar fringe of society to their eternal salvation. He said he had visited the dark side and had witnessed it within himself.

I admired his boldness and courage to serve God wherever he was being led. The thing that hooked me early with my deceiver was the idea that collectively we would serve God by guiding the lost and hopeless to eternal salvation. Beyond that was the belief that we had been called directly by God to do this type of work. In fact, it was through reincarnation he argued that we had returned to earth to complete the mission. You see, my deceiver proclaimed me to be an "old soul," too. According to him, I had "walked with Jesus" in a previous lifetime. So in our (re)union, we were really just getting the old band back together to serve humanity in this most critical turning point in the spiritual evolution of religions all over the world.

I was not conditioned to believe in reincarnation. I had never in my life contemplated that idea before. But under the influence of the evil one, I was too ignorant to resist. I'll admit, it felt really good to hear that I "walked with Jesus" in another lifetime and that I was called into this purpose. I was seeking. I was ready to go to war for my Father in Heaven. So I didn't properly vet the false teachings. I assumed the role because it fed both my heart and perhaps my ego as well. If reincarnation was possible, I really didn't believe that my life would ever take on any greater significance. So I was ready to go all in and prove my faith.

Once the concept had fully taken root within me, however, the devil turned the knife. In a moment of pure vulnerability, I shared with him openly something very personal that I had never spoken of to anyone else in my lifetime. It was a deep-rooted fear. An obsessive-compulsive negative thought that had persisted over many years. I could never understand its origin. That troubled me. In fact, I often blamed myself for the fear as though it was something for which I was responsible. I know now that it was the devil who had placed it there.

In seeking support to understand the nature of the fear and its root, the devil guided me back to the notion of reincarnation. He reminded me that my soul had survived many lifetimes. "I thought that I walked with Jesus," I said. How could I be carrying something with such an evil root? He affirmed that I had indeed walked with Jesus but that my soul also spent time in the Dark Ages. During that period of history, many were led to unspeakable evils, including myself.

He then proceeded to suggest to me the heinous crimes that I may have committed in that previous lifetime. I was moved to sickness. I didn't want to believe it. But the principle of reincarnation meant that it was very possible. So if I wanted to accept the notion that I walked with Jesus, perhaps I also needed to believe that I once committed the most evil sins known to man.

The devil had turned the tables on me. He baited me and tempted me to feel into the idea of my soul's reincarnation by presenting it to be rooted in a former connection to Jesus. That was something I yearned for deeply. He knew it. So I bought the lie. Then later, as soon as it had settled into my heart, he perverted it with pure evil by indicating that I was once no better than he and his evil legion. I, too, was once a member of the most twisted segment of society.

The idea of reincarnation was working toward a number of aspects of Satan's grand scheme. As you'll see over the coming chapters, every single bad fruit is somehow connected to each of the others. The reduction of Jesus, the bait-and-switch tactics, and the ongoing desensitization toward all things evil were themes that began to show themselves over and over again throughout our relationship. There was not a single lie that wasn't serving another scheme.

In describing the evil one, I like to use this parable: "Every morning, the spider weaves its web." The web of deception is thick and intricate. Even though one morning you may blow through it without getting sidetracked, you can rest assured that the very next day, another even grander web of lies will be waiting for you. The devil is relentless. He is always hunting his prey. It takes great perseverance to withstand his advances and reveal his schemes.

CHAPTER 12

THE BAD FRUIT

DESENSITIZATION

Woe to those who call evil good and good evil, who put darkness for light and light for darkness, who put bitter for sweet and sweet for bitter. (Isaiah 5:20)

IN MY FIRST ENCOUNTER WITH THE DEVIL, HE DIS-guised himself as a devout follower of Jesus Christ. Looking back, I can see now that he embodied the type of faith that lacked any real backbone. It was very much a surface-level representation. It was rooted in the prosperity gospel. At that stage of my life, it resonated. My journey as a believer was just beginning, and my faith had not yet had the opportunity to fully ripen. I was still a surface-level follower of Christ, and I believed that I could blend the desires of my flesh with my religion. I was vulnerable to the apostasy. The devil knew that very well.

In the years that followed, I exposed the lies of the prosperity gospel. So in his second pursuit, the devil adapted his motives. His evolved mission wasn't to simply lead me into the betrayal of my Father via the temptation of money but rather to capture my soul. In round two, he presented his faith as syncretic. This meant that he followed a blend of deities, beliefs, and practices. I was okay with the fact that he was not solely Christian because I was finding many areas where we were seemingly aligned. Further, he proclaimed to me that he recognized Jesus as a key figure in his spiritual journey. On the surface, he did not attempt to openly steer me away from Him, though this was, of course, part of the deception that I would reveal later.

As I mentioned previously, the devil won the opening round. I desired greater freedom, and I sought it through the things of the world. I ignored every signal from the Spirit that was in opposition, and I trudged forward on the path to captivity like a pig being led to slaughter. I followed a gospel that I knew was dishonest simply because it aligned with the desires of my flesh. I wanted a home where I felt comfortable. I didn't care to see the error of my ways.

By the time of his second approach, I had discovered the nature of my missteps, and I had exposed the false doctrine that had led me back to countless seasons of suffering in lack. I was fed up with the lies of the world. I was looking for a fight.

During the initial conversations in our reunion, the devil and I discussed how the world was preparing to undergo a radical shift. Life as we had known it was not going to continue much longer. It simply couldn't. As a Christian, this led me to further analysis of the Book of Revelation. Many signals had already begun pointing to the End Times and (per my beliefs) the eventual return of Jesus Christ. My research sparked additional curiosity within me regarding the last days. I wanted to understand the dark forces of both the natural and spiritual worlds that had long been at odds with God.

Beyond my curiosity regarding the coming apocalypse, I was very interested in understanding what types of demonic forces had been infiltrating my soul. You see, I had recently undergone a meditative "healing" session with my deceiver. During that session, we had allegedly detached something dark. In my mind's eye, I witnessed it. I was led into an altered state of consciousness where I saw a huge dark mass hovering over me. As I spoke to it, it turned to face me, and soon after, it was commanded by my "healer" to leave. But who or what was it exactly?

The answer that I was given was "Satan." Yikes. Satan, that's a little creepy. But "Don't worry," my deceiver advised, Satan was just "the matrix" or our worldly prison here on earth. There were far more dangerous demons lurking out there in the spiritual world. He knew all of them. In fact, he could describe them all in great detail. Oh, and that guy Lucifer, don't worry about him either. That's just your ego. In fact, he assured me that he and Lucifer had a great relationship with each other. All of that stuff that I had been taught about him, that was nonsense.

The devil worked quickly to expose me to all of the spiritual forces that he declared were in opposition of the Light. In altered states of consciousness, he had encountered all kinds of dark entities. He spoke to me about the reptilian-like creatures that had visited him at night. Disturbingly, he was able to identify each and every one of them by name.

He embodied a radical awareness of all things, even the darkest things. Within him, there was this undeniable yearning to seek and understand every demonic presence and dark experience of life on a deeper level, including death itself. He had once even used transcendental meditation to travel and navigate his way through the human experience of death out of his own curiosity. He boasted of his ability to return, given that most humans are not equipped to make that journey and come back from it.

It was all quite fascinating to me, although much of it was beyond my ability to fully comprehend. My desire was simply to be able to identify the dark forces of evil so that I could expose them in the Light. The devil, of course, understood the demonic forces of the spiritual world quite intimately because he communed with them. They were under his care. Blinded by deception, I brazenly adopted the belief that he would be a great resource to draw from as I began navigating the darkness in my own mission.

Now, the devil is the prince of darkness. Most of us know that quite well. But in his grand deception, he masquerades as a false light that is in opposition to the Light of God. In God, there is no darkness at all. Satan, however, cannot hide his dark roots. At least not completely. He can't help but show his hand. Yet, it can be difficult as a human caught up in sin to reveal it. In a sense, we can all relate. Every person walking this earth has faced the darkness at varying times throughout their life. The darkness is often the catalyst that leads us to a fuller embracing of *the* Light. So Satan's deceptive message of feigned redemption resonates. We can relate because we once were of him.

When my deceiver spoke to me about the dark beings present in his past, I believed him. I thought perhaps they were in mine as well. Maybe I just didn't have the eyes to see them at the time. But I sensed that my evolving mission in faith may require me to confront them more openly in the future. So I wanted to be more aware. I admired the stillness that my deceiver was able to embody in speaking to me about evil. He could sit comfortably while staring down the darkness and subduing it. I believed that was evidence of the power of the Light within him. On the surface, it appeared divinely offered. I wanted to align with it.

Let's look back to the "bad fruit" of reincarnation for a moment. You'll recall that I mentioned the evil one sharing with me elements of his soul journey that were horrific in nature. This was a calculated effort at desensitization. He was laying the groundwork so that when I had fully embraced the idea of my own old soul, he could twist the knife inside of me by suggesting that I, too, had committed heinous crimes against humanity in a past life. He knew that in seeking to uncover the answers to questions that I could not resolve within the framework of this lifetime, I would become more heavily reliant on him to fill in the holes remaining in my story (areas that I couldn't access in my conscious mind). I would need to revisit "memories" that I could only access through the guidance of transcendental meditation. I would need to surrender to his will. To be led. He presented it as though there was really no other choice if I truly wanted to move forward in my faith journey. It was a masterful scheme. Every piece was connected.

Where I believed that I was gaining knowledge and useful insight to prepare me for the mission that I was being called to serve, I was instead being deliberately desensitized and led to submission according to his will. Evil was becoming normalized. It wouldn't be long before I was communing with it, perhaps in stillness, that being the ultimate goal. But did I really want to sit and be still in a room full of demons? How long would it be until that comfort led to acceptance and then attachment? If I allowed myself to embrace the notion of reincarnation and the suggestion that the darkest and most profound forms of evil were attached to my soul, then what in my own self-seeking forgiveness might I be willing to tolerate both inside of myself and elsewhere? The devil once told me that there would be a day when I would learn to forgive and honor Lucifer. Is that where I was headed?

CHAPTER 13

THE BAD FRUIT

THE DARK LEGION

He who dwells in the shelter of the Most High will abide in the shadow of the Almighty. I will say to the Lord, "My refuge and my fortress, my God, in whom I trust." For he will deliver you from the snare of the fowler and from the deadly pestilence. He will cover you with his pinions, and under his wings you will find refuge; his faithfulness is a shield and buckler. You will not fear the terror of the night, or the arrow that flies by day, nor the pestilence that stalks in darkness, nor the destruction that wastes at noonday. (Psalm 91:1–6)

IT BECAME CLEAR TO ME DURING THE EARLY STAGES OF my second encounter with the devil that he had a vested interest in acquiring intimate knowledge of both the spiritual entities that served him and the followers he had amassed in the natural world. I myself was familiar with a handful of dark entities referenced in Scripture: Satan/Lucifer, Baal,

Beelzebub, and so forth. But there were countless others spoken of to me by the evil one that had never crossed my radar. Many of them were beings that you would not hear of anywhere else. Some reportedly visited my deceiver personally, and others he communed with through transcendental meditation. Again, this was all quite normal to him. Most would see it as reckless, but I excused it as fearlessness in faith. His ability to go to dark places and return unscathed intrigued me because I had a sincere desire to hold a similar power in the face of evil. I wanted to be able to confront demonic forces without hesitancy and intimidation and bring them to the Light of Jesus Christ. That type of divine mission really aligned perfectly with the warrior mentality that I had embraced for all of my life.

In round two with the devil, the desensitization process started early. It began with my own meditative healing session, which then led to further education about the dark forces of the spiritual realm. The demonic beings crash course that I was offered as part of the devil's desensitization effort was the exact awareness that I needed to release the activity I soon began experiencing inside of my home. It should perhaps be no surprise that as it became "normal" for me to anticipate the presence of dark beings, I began to see them show up all around me. In a sense, I was inviting them in. My "awareness" opened the door. Think back to the story of Adam and Eve in the Garden of Eden. This was the awareness of evil.

As I grew closer in alignment with the devil's deception, the energy in my home during the nighttime hours began to shift quite dramatically. Two days after the meditative "healing" session in which I confronted a dark mass and (supposedly) detached it from my being, I experienced an absolutely torturous night of sleep. I was in and out of intense nightmares until at least 3:00 a.m. Dark forces were attempting to prey on my mind as I sought rest and resisted with prayer, affirmations, and heart-centered breathing. My contention was that the demonic entities did not want to see me awakened. They recognized that I was on the verge of a spiritual breakthrough, and they wanted to send me back to bondage. My deceiver advised that I had essentially been switched on like a light and that the opposing forces were likely stirred up by that. The evil spirits simply were coming around to check on me. He urged me not to worry because they really couldn't do any harm. They were just curious.

For protection, I was advised to utilize a couple of prayers that were shared at the conclusion of the healing session. I was also offered some shielding meditation music, which did help me restore my calm temporarily in the moments when I felt troubled. But in my heart, I remained unsettled.

I began to feel a rising urge to "test the spirits." I was open to growing in faith, but I had no desire to deviate from my path to Jesus. So I reaffirmed my position as a devoted Christian. My deceiver confirmed that he was perfectly fine with that. He also revealed that (though he followed a syncretic religion) he walked with Christ as his spirit guide. He even went so far as to share with me the armor of God to use in prayer. Then he encouraged me not to allow dogma to blind me but rather to look for the common bonds and leave the rest to God.

Despite his reassurance, however, the activity in our home at nighttime only continued to increase. One thing that became very noticeable was the disruption in the sleep patterns of our children. My son began having an extremely difficult time falling asleep, and throughout the night, he began waking frequently. Even as I implemented nightly prayers of protection outside of the doors of my children at bedtime, things seemed to only get worse. My infant daughter, who was born in October of 2019, also began waking more frequently, although her disruption was quite a bit less pronounced.

There wasn't much that was going to shake me. But I will admit that I found the activity around my children to be extremely disturbing. I could handle the darkness, but I was not okay with demons visiting my son and daughter. Repeatedly, the risk of this type of interference was downplayed by my deceiver to be something of no great significance or consequence. Here again, desensitization was at work. This was all normal. No big deal.

Yet, I seemed to recall a conversation when my deceiver had

revealed a similar type of disruption that had occurred in the home of another acquaintance of his following a "healing" session. Details were not shared about the activity, but I do remember the twisted nature of the remedy he applied. A drop of blood was given to Lucifer as an offering to put an end to the disturbance. Lucifer. Yes, the same Lucifer labeled simply as the ego, the fallen angel who (according to my deceiver) was not Satan, but rather a less threatening being whom I would later "learn to forgive and honor." Lucifer was the recipient of the blood offering. A blood offering to cease dark spiritual activity around children. Yet, somehow in my case, the threat wasn't ever of any concern? This didn't add up. Was this another desensitization effort? At some point down the road, would I be advised to give my blood to the devil to put an end to the activity in my own home? If I forgave and honored Lucifer, who knows what I may be led to do.

One night, my wife and I were having a very deep spiritual conversation as we were lying in bed with each other. You could say that I was pushing the envelope a bit in working to get her to open up. We were doing some powerful reflection. I could sense her "activation" as we began to uncover some hidden memories that had served as limiting beliefs in her life for quite some time. It was a very intimate dialogue.

In a room completely void of light, I watched a dark shadow move across the wall to our right. Keep in mind that we have blackout curtains in our bedroom, so this was not a shadow caused by light coming through a window. I recognized its nature immediately, and I was not afraid. I was ready to bring the fight to it, particularly after the disturbances that I had been witnessing with our children.

Moments later, I felt that the presence had moved to the middle of our ceiling by the fan. It was hovering there above the bed, a dark and cloudy mass. At this point, my wife was able to see it as well. I told her that I felt as though it was placing a weight over my eyelids, a feeling that you might encounter with an approaching migraine. There was also a visual distortion that came upon me in the moment that was likely quite similar to what one might experience with cataracts.

Years earlier, I would have shivered with anxiety in the midst of this type of experience. But in this moment, I appreciated the challenge that it was affording me. I called on my "training" to remain still, and I calmed my wife's nerves, using my prayers of protection to drive the dark mass away. As I stared at the shadow defiantly and spoke words of Light-embodied resistance, it slowly dissipated before leaving us completely.

In reflection, I sensed that something was preying upon my wife's soul and that it really didn't like the idea of me opening her up. After all, we had gone through an extraordinarily similar experience with each other many years earlier (several months before my first encounter with the devil) that unfolded in an almost identical fashion. Back then, I was a little shook up and intimidated. This time, I felt ready. Bring it on. Perhaps, I thought, this would be the season where the love of my life would truly be set free.

A week or so after the event in our bedroom, my wife experienced a more targeted dark encounter that shook her up quite a bit. She was downstairs with our children. It was late in the afternoon, and I was up on the third floor finishing my workday. When I came down the stairs to have dinner with the family, she described a startling occurrence to me. She explained that she was standing at the edge of the living room when something caused her to turn toward the stairs. In doing so, she saw a dark shadow in the form of a human move at the banister, almost as if it was tiptoeing down to check on her. The moment it recognized that she noticed its presence, it vanished in a flash. She told me that she initially believed it to be me. When she realized that couldn't be the case because I was still working two floors above her, she became extremely frightened.

Something dark was working to retain its influence over my wife. I was convinced of it. Outside of the evidence presenting itself in moments when we were together or when she was alone, there were the signals that I began seeing in my time apart from her as well.

One night, my wife and I were discussing some of the inner-child healing work that I had been doing as we made our way to the bedroom. Following that conversation, I had a strong sense that she could benefit from the same exercise. So, as she was getting ready for bed, I encouraged her to give it a try sometime soon as I said "Good night" and left the room, making my way downstairs to finish up a few things before I retired for the evening as well. As I walked into the kitchen, I had a sense that something was watching me. I felt as though I needed to keep looking over my shoulder, but there was nothing there.

A little while later, I sat down on the couch and began thinking back on our conversation. Soon after, I saw clear as day in my mind's eye a vision of my wife standing at the top of the stairs in our home. She was black and white and looked to be about ten or more years younger. I could feel the pain of her shadow deep in my heart. She was silent and appeared to be mute. It was almost as if she had been pulled out of a dark basement where the light had not been able to reach her. Here she was, standing in front of me, so much pain buried deep inside but lacking the words to describe it.

I ran upstairs to tell my wife about the experience, and I implored her to do the inner-child work soon. I believed that my vision was a sign for what would be a critical step in a breakthrough season that could truly help to place her on a path to set her soul free. But my share only seemed to shake her up even more. Strangely, it all felt very normal to me. I was okay with acknowledging my shadow. That was easy in the face of far more formidable demons. I had been desensitized.

To her, my visions weren't things that she was all that prepared to see. Perhaps she was frightened by the idea of what she may uncover in doing the work. Maybe with good reason. I paused and stepped away. I came to understand that everything would reveal itself in due time. As it arrived, I trusted that we would draw on the strength of the Father to deal with it together, as a family.

As crazy as it sounds, I began to feel that I could reason through all of the dark interference that was becoming visible in our home. I was growing comfortable with it. That was until the night that I encountered something in my son's room that truly shook me up. He had just lain down, and he was having an awful time getting settled. My wife had been in and out of the room numerous times, and nothing she had tried seemed to be making a difference. At one point, I decided to go in to check on him. I stepped to his door, and immediately after cracking the threshold, I smelled sulfur. I got a very sick feeling in my stomach.

I knew what that smell signaled in the spiritual realm: the pit of hell. I was really hoping that it wasn't that. Perhaps it was simply a trick of my senses? Maybe it would dissipate quickly? I waited for a few minutes. It persisted. I left the room and returned several times, and in the same area by the door, the smell remained. I didn't know what to do. So I heaped a load of prayers on my son and on our home. Thankfully, we made it through the night. By the next morning, it was gone.

When I brought this to the attention of my deceiver, he used it as motivation to tell me that I really needed to take the next step in my spiritual evolution and draw into closer relationship with him. How could I set out on a path to teach and heal anyone else while I was still dealing with sulfur in my own home?

This event was a dagger. The devil was fully aware of how much I hated the idea of demons messing with my children. I could no longer live in denial of their presence. In the past, when I wanted to remain oblivious to the threat of dark entities approaching my kids, I could always explain away their restless nights as simply the evolving disruption of sleep cycles in infants and toddlers. But this experience with sulfur cut me deep. This was directed at my son. My miracle from God. For the first time, it wasn't quickly dismissed as insignificant. It was an experience that the evil one wanted me to recognize as a threat. That was clear.

Satan is a master of the setup. He desensitized me to the point where I began accepting the presence of his evil legion within my home. He led me to believe there was no reason to worry by empowering me in the face of darkness. Then he turned the tables on me, seeking to prey upon my most pronounced "weakness," which was my desire to protect my family. In doing so, he shifted me from a position of confident spiritual fortitude back to a state of vulnerable submission and reliance on his wisdom. In my weakness, he dug his claws in deeper.

CHAPTER 14

THE BAD FRUIT

SEXUAL IMMORALITY

Flee from sexual immorality. All other sins a person commits
are outside the body, but whoever sins sexually, sins against
their own body. Do you not know that your bodies are temples
of the Holy Spirit, who is in you, whom you have received
from God? You are not your own; you were bought at a price.
Therefore honor God with your bodies. (1 Corinthians 6:18–20)

MANY PEOPLE WILL ARGUE THAT THE DEVIL IS NOT
Lucifer, that they are two separate spiritual beings. They
will contend that Lucifer is "the morning star" or the "Light
Bringer" rather than Satan ("The Adversary"). I wrestled
with this deception for quite some time. Ultimately, I landed
on what I now believe to be an undeniable truth. A truth
that became very clear to me as I reflected on the sexual
perversion of the deceiver that I encountered. Lucifer and
Satan are one and the same—the devil.

Although enlightenment and the ascension to a higher state of consciousness dominated the doctrine of my deceiver (very specifically Luciferian in nature), there was always a very dark sexual undertone that he could not keep hidden. Call it almost an obsession.

Have you ever met an addict? Take a compulsive gambler, for example. If they've been a slave to their habit for any period of time, they will have a very difficult time hiding their master. I know this because I once lived this lifestyle. Jesus tells us that "the mouth speaks what the heart is full of" (Matthew 12:34), so when you hear a gambling addict speaking about his recent trip to Vegas or his local poker game, his heart reveals his obsession via his tongue. He can't help but speak about it. It's become the central focus of his existence. He has begun to put his addiction on a pedestal and worship it like a god. His darkness cannot be hidden.

On the surface, my deceiver appeared very loyal to the idea of pure, heart-centered, and light-guided intention. At the time, that appealed to me. But ultimately, I learned that my Light (the Light of God) was not his light. His light was Luciferian in nature. It was at odds with my True Light.

This disconnect was extremely hard to identify for quite some time. I was, however, aware of this truth—at odds with God's Light is sexual immorality. That is a point that has never been up for debate. Satan's perversion of the sacred act of sex has long been a mark of his evil ministry. Like the gambler, he can't help but speak about it. He is obsessed with it, and not sex in its pure form, but sex in the way of the wicked and dark. If you want to identify the evil one and draw a line in the sand between the Light of God and the deceptive light of Lucifer, be a witness to how the devil speaks about sex.

Very early into our second encounter, it became clear to me that one thing my deceiver could not disguise was his insatiable appetite for sex. He often spoke about it like a teenage boy. At times, I could almost visualize him salivating as he recalled his conquests of women and revealed his perversions. He knew that his language made me very uncomfortable, and yet, even as I repeatedly made efforts to divert his comments, he continued to push them on me in an extremely egotistical manner. He always made humor of it because he had this idea that I was a prude. He repeatedly asserted that in time, he would open me up to a world of gratifying sexual pleasure beyond my imagination, once I became "fully activated." He pitched this because he believed that it would motivate me to align more closely with him when in reality it was one of the areas that gave me the most pause.

Sex caused me to really question the sanctity of my deceiver's spiritual healing methods, as in time, I came to understand that nearly all of his intimate encounters seemed to originate in settings where there was presumed trust and safety established in the spirit of faith. Women were a marked target. That was clear. The evil one had a way of tempting them with spiritual freedom and coercing them into submission and romantic entanglement. In many cases, he was preying upon known vulnerabilities. Perhaps it was the lack of guidance from a strong father figure on earth combined with a lack of understanding of the love of the Father in Heaven.

My deceiver often spoke as though women threw themselves at him because they could not resist his aura. This was his way of denying any responsibility to me, his Christian acquaintance who would clearly be disturbed by his actions. But I wasn't blind. I didn't need to see his methods firsthand to know what he was doing. He would draw them in with faith, open them up, release their inhibitions, convince them that sex offered in "free will" was an expression of pure love and light and then become their master. Later, when they fell into the error of their ways, he would detach from them, paint them as "dark," and allow them to live in the guilt and shame that in many cases had led them to seek healing in the first place. This type of painful detachment then promoted the very same cycle of sexual oppression that the victim had likely been desperately seeking to break. It reinforced their captivity.

I spent many hours in conversation with my deceiver about the very real sexual perversion underlying our society. Part of what motivated me to go deeper in my journey with him was this idea that the veil would ultimately be removed and abusive acts of sexual immorality would be exposed. He led me to believe that I would be the steady hand of faith when the world awakened to the disclosure of sex trafficking, pedophilia, ritualistic abuse, and so forth. My understanding was that I would serve as a guide for those completely overwhelmed by the chaos of this type of grand reveal of evil. I would stand with God in the Light and be a beacon for people to turn to in the midst of all the darkness. It made sense, and it aligned with my research on the End Times. It was an honorable, faith-rooted mission, I thought.

Over time, I came to sense that our paths were diverging. He viewed this unveiling by the light as necessary for enlightenment only (see Eve's temptation in the Garden of Eden, for example), whereas I saw the Light as essential for exposure AND justice.

At one point, evidence was shared regarding arrests that were being made, which would contribute to society's grand reveal in the realm of sexual immorality and pedophilia. I was thrilled to see the headlines as I stated in victory, "Bring the evil to the Light," and prepared for the next sequence of events to unfold. That's when things got really weird. In anticipation of my deceiver's agreement, I was shocked to hear him respond, "No evil, all is light," as he told me to "let go of judgment" and "love them all for they know not what they do."

Wait. No evil? My whole mission was rooted in the idea of exposing and fighting evil. What type of sick manipulation was this? I was disgusted. Just when things couldn't seemingly get any stranger, he went on to make the chilling statement that I have referenced several times already in "there will be a time you will forgive and honor Lucifer."

I challenged him immediately, and he pushed back with poetic discourse, speaking in terms of dimensionality that would make anyone's head explode. So ultimately, I stepped away but with a very cautious demeanor. I knew that my Father drew a distinct line between good and evil, and perhaps in no place was that more evident than in the realm of sexual immorality, particularly with children. There was no chance that I was ever going to abstain from calling such heinous acts evil. I was not going to endorse anyone's freedom from God's judgment. I knew that we were all going to be called to answer for our actions on the day that we met our Maker. No person or entity was going to convince me otherwise.

CHAPTER 15

THE BAD FRUIT

DESERTION AND LACK

Fear the Lord, you his holy people, for those who fear him lack nothing. The lions may grow weak and hungry, but those who seek the Lord lack no good thing. (Psalm 34:9–10)

THE DEVIL WAS A MAGNET IN HIS COURTSHIP. HE HAD this ability to manipulate his energy in such a way that you couldn't help but want to learn more. In my first encounter, it was his confidence that was truly alluring. He embodied the excitement of the promise of financial freedom, and he convincingly paired that energy with the false doctrine of the prosperity gospel. In the weakness of my flesh, I bought in. I had long suffered under the weight of debt. And I believed that in my rebirth, God was going to bless me in my pursuits beyond my wildest imagination. I was due. This was going to be my time. Or so I thought anyway.

When reality did finally hit me between the eyes, I was stunned. I felt a level of betrayal that I had never experienced at any point in my life. It was nothing like the betrayal of a lover or a friend. It was far deeper than that. This was the realization that I had been scammed by an imposter of Christ. I began to understand the shame of my decisions in aligning with such an entity, and I felt fierce anger toward the evil one. He played me. For years, I was going to be left picking up the pieces of my life that he had shattered as a result of his deception.

But I was no victim. The Spirit had warned me days before I went all in. The signal was undeniable. I felt the presence of evil in such a profound way that it made me ill. I knew I needed to turn away. But I didn't. I was blinded by the pursuit of money and the freedom that I believed it could afford me. My flesh would not let it go. So I aligned my talents with an opportunity that left me both spiritually and financially empty. I deserved the consequences of my actions.

The devil can manipulate his energy to a point. In his seductive advance, it's easy to be deceived because it's in our nature to want to believe. But when questions begin to flare about his motives and the Word of God begins circulating in his presence, the true nature of the evil one becomes visible. Sadly, we sometimes need to go deeper in relationship with him in order to see it, but it's there. You can't hide pure darkness in the presence of God's Light.

Choosing not to see the evil in my first encounter was shameful because it wasn't solely the conviction of the Spirit. There were several other signals as well. I had witnessed the deep lack that my deceiver embodied, and I listened to conversations where he referenced desertion from many other former supporters. I knew those things were not of God. Certainly by aligning my journey with his, I was not going to allow God's blessings to unfold in my life. Yet, I looked the apostasy dead in the eyes and went forward anyway. Was there really any greater sin than that?

The answer is, perhaps. If my Father were to give me another chance to resist the evil one and I failed to turn away yet again, that would seriously deteriorate our relationship. Perhaps this time, for eternity. This was serious business. I needed the Lord's discipline to prepare me for the day that I reconvened with my enemy. That's why for years, I went into training in preparation.

When the devil arrived in my life for the second time, it was again his energy that moved me into a closer relationship with him. This time it had nothing to do with any talk of prosperity but rather a stillness in the midst of chaos. It was his calming presence that appealed to me. That's the persona I wanted to embody both in the mental health community and in my faith. I wanted to know "how can you assist me with a personal transformation that will allow me to be more like you?" I shudder now at the danger of that statement, but at the time, that's what my ignorance desired.

Many were drawn into the presence of my deceiver, led seemingly by the same energetic attraction that had appealed to me. But it routinely appeared that there was something that turned them off as they got closer. Over time, I learned that desertion was beginning to occur with great frequency among many of his followers. In response to that desertion, my deceiver spent a considerable amount of time tearing down the abandoners.

The devil would tell me about the very personal experiences that he had with each of his defectors. His ego couldn't help but boast about how they had done such wonderful work together. But he would ultimately conclude that the individual got cornered by religious dogma, by fear, or perhaps by a persistent block that they did not wish to resolve. Those things were what led them to make the decision to turn away from his influence.

He was deeply offended by the resistance. His common response to those who abandoned him was to sort of shun them until the time that they willingly cracked the door back open. Many did not reengage, but some did. In the rare case when that occurred, my deceiver would employ a very aggressive reengagement approach. Almost a "how dare you?" type of attitude.

To me, this didn't feel like love at all. My deceiver, who was supposedly deeply rooted in the Light, sure seemed to spend a whole lot of time dwelling in anger and resentment. I remember advising him countless times to "knock the dust off your feet and move on." "Not everyone is a win or a loss; some are rain checks." "Plant the seed and see if it takes root." These ideas made sense to me because they were beliefs rooted in my study of Scripture and the ministry of Jesus. Although he acted as though he embraced them upon receipt, his resentment only continued to fester. He couldn't avoid speaking about the dissention. He was always adding enemies to his list.

With so many people resisting his advanced training, my initial contention was that most people weren't truly willing to go deep in their faith. In other words, it was comfortable to preach faith and to act as though you were fully bought in, but actually living it was a completely different ball game. Let's be honest, this is the sad truth of many believers today. Living in pure faith isn't easy, and it's not for the faint of heart.

My understanding was that when fellow followers of my deceiver had been invited to take the next step in their spiritual evolution, they arrived (as I did) at a point where they had a decision to make. Either go all in, or turn back. Unlike most others, I pushed forward because I had been fooled into believing that I was doing so in an act of a more committed faith to my Lord and Savior, Jesus Christ. Those who were more careful remained a bit guarded in stepping out into the unknown. Knowing what I do now, I can't blame them for that at all. I am writing this book as a result of what I discovered beyond the wall of resistance. It wasn't pretty.

My deceiver was always keeping records of wrongs or slights against him. I continuously sought ways to justify his behavior because I wasn't prepared to see what I needed to see in him. I wanted to believe that the collective mission that we found ourselves on was genuine. That it was rooted in the Truth and that it would ultimately draw me closer to God.

Out of respect, I began accepting many of the labels that the devil assigned to those who had abandoned his false doctrine. In my heart, resentment began taking root. I started to frame that segment of society as weak, and I began distancing myself from the social circles that were in resistance to our message. Because I felt that in a sense, I was above them. They weren't living faith; they were floundering. I believed that I was ascending beyond their level of understanding, so I didn't care to waste any more time or energy entertaining them. They would only hold me back. I had a far more important mission to fulfill. I wanted to seek those who were willing to see, not those who were stuck in resistance. The ironic thing is that it was me who truly couldn't see.

Many stories were shared by my deceiver relating to his followers' dissention. Within them, there were a couple of departing messages that he referenced that deeply plagued my heart. I kept repeating them over and over in my mind. What did these people mean when they offered these comments? Where were they at in their spiritual journeys when they decided to break the chain of deceit?

Knowing what I do now, these messages are chilling to recount. The first related to a follower's discomfort with complete surrender to my deceiver. Yes, surrender. I thought of Jesus in the wilderness as the devil said, "All this I will give to you if you bow down and worship me" (Matthew 4:9). There was a conclusiveness to it. This wasn't just an experiment. Clearly, the finality had led to serious apprehension.

The second message was in regard to a follower's decision to step away from the relationship and choose the devil that they knew. This statement was also extraordinarily powerful because it revealed the deception. There had to be a whole lot of confusion and mistrust present. Although the true nature of the evil one may not have been fully revealed, something didn't seem right to this individual about my deceiver. So a retreat was made, and it likely was crafted despite the devil's warning that it would result in the adherence to an established pattern of destructive beliefs that were rooted in old conditioning.

Perhaps the most troubling aspect of all of this was the fact that my deceiver did not hesitate to share these very specific parting remarks with me. In the midst of all of the deception, he was essentially revealing his true nature boldly with arrogance, and I disregarded it because I was so blinded by all of the other brainwashing he had applied to me. At this point, an outsider may have questioned, was the devil really hiding from me, or was I hiding the devil?

In a similar fashion to our first encounter, I also began to recognize that my deceiver was again operating from a place of severe lack. He survived off manipulation, and he promised others things through relationships with him that he could never himself attain or embody. The lack was hard to understand because this was one of the smartest and most adept beings I had ever encountered. He understood a vast array of disciplines quite intimately. Seemingly, he could have chosen any vocation and hit home runs. Here he was, sitting in lack and chasing the mysteries of his faith. I guess perhaps in a way, I admired the courage that it took to do that. I also questioned why God had not yet chosen to bless his path.

My personal belief is that if I am true to my calling; I can trust that, like a magnet, I will attract the right people, the right opportunities, and the right outcomes to my life. This is the core essence of my living faith. If the Light of Christ shines in me, it will reveal the path that I am called to follow, and doors will open along the way as I continue to step forward in complete reliance on my Creator and Savior. I believe that the Lord will care for my needs just as He does for "the birds of the air" (Matthew 6:26). When I remain in alignment with His Truth, the worries of the world fade away. And God provides.

In the case of my deceiver, this dependence on the Father did not exist. His survival hinged on manipulation. To me, that was evidence that he was not seeking God.

Eerily, the lack did not seem to bother him. Perhaps partly because his negotiated comforts were admittedly pretty nice. He once told me that he didn't believe his work was going to be tied to money. He had made peace with that. To be honest, I could relate to that notion, too, because I had also begun to feel a detachment from money. The interesting thing, however, is that as he began coercing me into a deeper relationship with him, he often reminded me just how much money I'd be able to make by administering the healing methods that he would be teaching me. Then he'd float the temptation of the size of the market that I'd have at my disposal. It apparently was a market that he himself could never successfully capture on his own.

My deceiver was preaching a false gospel of abundance by utilizing the same techniques that only led to his own embodiment of lack. He wanted me to define and sign a contract with him, ensuring my alignment with a similar fate. He knew that when I was drowning in lack and in debt, my faith starved as well. This was the biggest and most persistent worldly obstacle I had faced throughout my life. He knew that well because he had coordinated every single money-driven trap that I had fallen into since I had become an adult. He was committed to ensuring that I never escaped that pit of captivity because in the Light, I would truly shine. And his deception would finally be revealed.

CHAPTER 16

THE BAD FRUIT

LATE NIGHTS AND DAYTIME IDLENESS

This is the verdict: Light has come into the world, but people loved darkness instead of light because their deeds were evil. Everyone who does evil hates the light, and will not come into the light for fear that their deeds will be exposed. (John 3:19–20)

IN THE MONTHS LEADING UP TO MY REBIRTH IN CHRIST, I dealt with an absolutely crippling panic disorder. A nervous breakdown had left me severely vulnerable. Anxiety began to overwhelm me like a flood, leading me into a state of agoraphobia. I was being swept away by the vicious current of mental illness. I was struggling to keep my head above water.

I entered that season of my life with about a decade of experience confronting anxiety and panic. Naturally, I sought to rely on the techniques that I had developed in those earlier periods of my mental health journey to survive. Those techniques helped me to a point. I got better at handling my personal demons throughout the day, but I did so primarily by manipulating my environment and removing any potential triggers. Ultimately, my desire for control was a big part of what influenced me to close off the world outside of my comfort zone, and that decision led me deeper into the captivity of my agoraphobia.

Nighttime was a nightmare. While asleep, I relinquished the control that I maintained during my waking hours. That's when my demons went to work. With great frequency, I would be drawn out of rest by panic attacks. Generally, they would occur about thirty to forty minutes into my sleep. I would lunge out of my sheets and onto the floor, yelling in terror and gasping for air. In every instance, I felt as though I was dying. It was terrifying. Some nights, I'd suffer through this experience as many as four or five times.

It got to the point that I began to fear and resist sleep altogether. I could sense the presence of my demons surrounding me as I drew the covers to my chest each night. I couldn't bear to put myself through the personal hell of the relentless attacks over and over again. So some nights, I stayed up to see the sunrise. I'd doze off for an hour or two and then head to my office and begin my workday. It was a sad way to live. The sleep deprivation took a tremendous toll on my body and my psyche.

I reference personal demons here several times, and I do so with great intention. My purpose is not to say that all mental illness is rooted in demonic influence. But from my current vantage point, I can tell you with great certainty that nearly every aspect of my battle was heavily affected by the work of Satan. Faith and faith alone healed me. So there is no doubt in my mind that the war I was fighting was on spiritual ground. It wasn't until I started treating it as such that I began to heal.

I learned from the experiences of my past that the devil loves to do his work at night. This is not a myth or a story created for horror films. This is truly when his legion is most active. So if you are keeping late hours, you are playing right into his hands. The choices you make at nighttime are of critical importance.

I remember the very moment during my second encounter with the devil when his nighttime influence became most visible to me. I was seven days into a transformational fast, and I was feeling phenomenal. The day prior, I began a practice of rising just before sunrise to head out and spend some time in solitude with God. As the Lord's brilliant Light began to paint the sky and the world around me awakened, I started running and making an intentional effort to soak in His perfect creation in deep reflection, prayer, and praise. It was magical. I had never felt so close to the Creator in my entire life. I was determined to make the experience a part of my regular morning routine.

As evening approached, my intention was to head to bed early to ensure that I continued the momentum I was building in my faith journey. My alone time with the Father was my top priority heading into the new week. Once the kids retired for the night, I cleaned up a few things and got myself ready for bed, setting my alarm for 5:30 a.m.

I was just beginning to pull the covers up to my chest when my phone began to ring. It was my deceiver. We hadn't spoken for several days live, although I had shared a few messages with him mainly because I felt like I was having one breakthrough after another in my early morning alone time with God. I was seeking validation for my surreal experiences in someone whom I thought would understand them better than anyone else I knew. But he was far less moved than I had anticipated. In a sense, he was almost indifferent or tuned out.

I remember wondering if perhaps he was threatened by what I was able to experience spiritually without his guidance. He often liked to remind me that I was not prepared for the depth of the journey that would unfold in my life. Here I was, guiding myself to surreal experiences on my own. I couldn't help but think that maybe that was a blow to his ego.

Looking back now, the timing of that ring sends chills up my spine. It was deliberate interference. When I saw the phone light up on the nightstand, I had an unsettled feeling about accepting the call. But I took it because I felt sort of compelled to do so. In conversation, I shared with him my genuine enthusiasm for the very intimate experiences I had been sharing with God. He said, "You sound clear," and then inquired about what I was doing. I told him I was heading to bed as my intention was to continue rising before the sun to dedicate my morning to a period of solitude with my Creator. He uttered a few words of support, but through his tone, I could sense his underlying anger and resentment. At the time, I attributed it to ego and perhaps the fear that he may lose me as a follower because I was giving him signals that I could lead my faith journey on my own. He wasn't going to let me go without a fight.

For the next few hours, my deceiver robbed me of precious time that I had planned to dedicate to rest and he coerced me to fall into deeper reliance on him. Now, obviously it takes two to tango, and I was an active participant in the conversation as well. But his demeanor and approach were beginning to really rub me the wrong way. The communication began to feel rather forceful. When I would challenge his position on something or question an idea that he was pushing on me, he became very defensive and condescending. I remember he repeatedly called me "dumb dumb" throughout our conversation. It seemed that he was dead set on puffing up his chest and revealing his spiritual superiority in an effort to convince me to remain dependent on him for my future evolution.

I could sense that my deceiver was desperate. He was backed into a corner because my faith was growing, and my relationship with Christ was beginning to outshine and outlast his advances. He knew it. It was now or never for him. Make a deal or lose me forever. So he went all in like never before.

Three and a half hours passed before I managed to pry myself away from the conversation. I walked to the bathroom and thought to myself, what in the world did I just do? Did I really gain anything from that discussion? Or did I simply sacrifice an opportunity to meet my Father for our planned date at dawn?

I'm sure that my deceiver walked away feeling as though he had won. But when my alarm went off at 5:30 a.m., I got up anyway. So what if I had only four hours of sleep? No big deal. I was going to honor my commitment to God. In doing so, I witnessed yet another amazing and miraculous sunrise, which served as proof that sometimes you just need to withstand the darkness until the morning comes. The dawn of the new day can serve as a beautiful reset.

As I began to reflect on the events of the night prior, I started to feel more deeply into this idea of timing. It really began to trouble me. I mean, it was literally as I was getting ready to switch off the lamp on my nightstand that the phone rang. I don't believe in coincidences. This disruption was orchestrated. It was an act against me to stymie the advancement of my early morning walk with the Father.

Looking back, I began to recall that many of the conversations I shared with my deceiver ran late into the night. Not all but quite a few. Nighttime was really the only period of the day that I had alone to myself while my wife and children were both asleep. So I excused the timing initially. I thought to myself, a 10:00 p.m. call that runs to 10:30 p.m. or 11:00 p.m. is no big deal. But an 11:30 p.m. call that extends until 2:00 a.m., that's far more disruptive. Over time, the latter became more the norm than the exception.

I started to recognize that my deceiver operated very well at night. This was when he was most active. He was not an early riser. In fact, he often spent a good portion of the day creating space for rest. We were diverging in this regard. I had learned from Scripture that Jesus was often active in the early hours before daybreak, and I was seeking to emulate that. When the sun went down, that was my signal to end the day. The devil, on the other hand, was just getting started. In the hours of darkness, his energy and techniques were most powerfully magnified. So naturally, that's when he made space for his work.

As I began to better understand my deceiver's nighttime habits, I also came to realize that our paths were diverging on idleness. Running had always served as a training ground of sorts in my life. More than the physical gains of exercise, I enjoyed the challenge of overcoming my mind. As I grew closer to God, I found that my appetite for activity also began to increase. So I sought to root that activity in Him. I began running differently. Not for my own gain but instead to create a quiet time for reflection, prayer, and praise. I started running longer and farther than ever before simply because I lost myself in it with the Father. It was deeply revealing and transformational.

To my deceiver, my running habits were extreme. He warned against too much physical exertion, and he encouraged me to do less. Just be "no exs" or "no excess or extremes" was the way that he described it. In a sense, I felt as though he was advising me to be weak and submissive. That did not align with my desires at all. I was seeking to become a bold warrior of Christ. I wanted to strengthen my vessel so that His message would never be made less impactful or become lost in any frailty that I embodied in the natural.

I knew very well that idleness left a person prone to the work of the devil. I had no intention of making myself a sitting duck for Satan. But that seemed to be the advice I was receiving more and more frequently as my relationship with my deceiver continued to evolve. Perhaps that was the reason he attempted to coerce me into late nights, to wear down my system and encourage me into accepting my own idleness throughout the day. He courted me with the idea that we would be the courageous light bearers when the darkness of the world was finally revealed, armed with hearts and minds built for spiritual warfare. As time went on, I found that he was leading me toward an idle submission and acceptance of all forces, both good and evil, for the achievement of the ultimate transcendence. I was not on board with that. My God drew a very clear line in the sand between good and evil. I wasn't going to sit idly in submission to anything that embodied an evil root, including him.

CHAPTER 17

THE BAD FRUIT

THE SHIFTING SHADOWS

Don't be deceived, my dear brothers and sisters. Every good
and perfect gift is from above, coming down from the Father of
the heavenly lights, who does not change like shifting shadows.
(James 1:16–17)

BY THE TIME OF MY SECOND MEETING WITH THE EVIL
one, I was heading into a period of great spiritual transformation. I had been working diligently to empty my vessel
and peel back the layers of my old conditioning so I could
be made new in Christ. And I began to feel led to engage
in some inner-child work to heal a few open wounds that
were rooted deep in my past.

My deceiver was on board with the idea and, in fact, had
been encouraging it. But he wanted me to seek him for
guided support with the meditation, likely because it would

serve as an opportunity for him to gain further access to areas of my subconscious mind where I was most vulnerable. I wanted to discover and speak to my inner child on my own time and under my own direction. This was a personal matter. I needed God to lead me to the healing and no one else.

I didn't have any training to fully understand how to navigate the healing, but I patiently worked my way through it really feeling into the needs and desires of the innocent voice within me. Through prayerful meditation, I began speaking openly to my inner child as if it were my own son or daughter that I was holding in my arms. In two visits, I found a new level of peace. It was an amazingly powerful experience.

As I uncovered my deepest wound, the abandonment, and inconsistency of the love that I had experienced throughout my lifetime, I felt my inner voice being guided back to the love of my Father in Heaven. I received a profound, divine message in the meditation that allowed me to release the pain of my childhood into peace within the arms of Jesus Christ, who I envisioned coming out of the sky to raise my childlike body and set me free. The message I received was, "His love is consistent."

God is our one true love. Every day when we wake up, He loves us with the very same compassion that He did the day before, despite our brokenness. Where love was lacking in the natural, there always remained the consistent love of the Father and the Son in the spiritual. God's love was enduring. It would never fade. Instead, it would continue to embrace me with each new morning for the rest of my life. I felt a warmth in that understanding that was deeply soothing to my inner child.

It was through my evolving understanding of the love and consistency of my Creator that I was able to identify yet another bad fruit within my deceiver. That was his chameleon-like nature. His inconsistency led me to the notion of "shifting shadows" referenced in Scripture. Specifically, in James 1:17, it reads, "Every good and perfect gift is from above, coming down from the Father of the heavenly lights, who does not change like shifting shadows."

If, in fact, my deceiver was as connected spiritually as he professed, thereby being nearer to God than most, why was he so wildly inconsistent in his messaging to me? His behavior did not in any way mirror the firmness of God's Truth that I had come to know in my life. In fact, it was quite the antithesis of that.

I had been courted by a charmingly heroic, light-embodied revolutionary. I was fascinated by him because my desire was to equip myself for battle with the darkness, both in the mental health community and in the spiritual realm. I had come to realize that the two were deeply intertwined, and I believed that if I could help an individual to uncover spiritual restoration, a superior mental well-being would be the natural by-product. It all made practical sense. The idea of winning the soul battle to embody the Light of God was one that truly resonated with me.

My deceiver understood my mindset. He planned his seduction accordingly. He wasted no time proclaiming to me that we were uniquely chosen as he advised that we were here to serve the people as the guides spoken of in the Book of Revelation, who would sing a new song before the throne. Very soon, the veil would be lifted. Humanity would become aware of the harsh reality that had been hidden from their view for centuries, the depths of all evil. God was going to expose it all, and His judgment was going to fall upon the earth, perhaps far sooner than anyone was anticipating.

For years, I had spent seasons of my life researching the darkness of society's underbelly. What I uncovered was absolutely nauseating. I could absorb it only in small doses; otherwise, it would keep me up all night long. It was hard for my natural mind to perceive such horrors. But I knew that it was real. I yearned to see God's justice be served.

Then into my life walked this prophet of sorts who assured me that everything I had prayed for was beginning to finally unfold. Beyond that, he led me to believe that I was placed on this earth to play a significant role for God in His final story. In the midst of all of the chaos, I would act as His trusted servant who would help to guide His children out of the overwhelming darkness and into the Light where they would find their eternal salvation.

As I mentioned previously, my deceiver had me convinced that I was an old soul. According to him, my soul, like his had survived many lifetimes in the natural, evolving over time to prepare for the moment when we would reunite the world with God. It seemed that perhaps the "hour unknown" was nearly upon us. If I was one of the 144,000 mentioned in the Book of Revelation as he had stated, I had a very serious mission to prepare for in the days ahead.

I recognize that it seems crazy to accept this type of disclosure as factual from anyone, but my deceiver had this "knowing" that was extraordinarily convincing. It was hard to deny that any of his poetically delivered revelations were false, even when they were things that you didn't care to see. So when he advised me that I was special, set apart, and called by God, my heart welcomed it. I had yearned to serve as a warrior in the army of Christ, so for me, his statements were simply confirmation that it was time to fully embrace the call.

With regard to the 144,000, in the literal sense, that was a bit hard for me to understand. My conclusion was that

I would be part of a community of believers who would stand tall in the End Times and lead millions of others to their salvation. Could there be a greater mission? I didn't believe so. The magnitude of my soul's perceived purpose began influencing every decision I made. It drew me closer to my deceiver who had revealed the designation because I really didn't think that anyone else could understand my spirituality on the level that he did.

That closeness was exactly what he desired. When you lean into the devil, he sinks his teeth into you. He needs your buy-in, and he works to acquire it through deception. Often completely unknowingly (as in my situation), we grant him the permission to begin directing our steps. We fall for the shiny surface allure and neglect to read the fine print. In an instant, he's got us hooked.

In an earlier chapter, I revealed to you that my deceiver was unnervingly comfortable with the dark. Although I embraced his courage, I couldn't help but question why he so actively sought it out. Seeking to me was far different than withstanding when confronted. Through transcendental meditation and altered states of consciousness, my deceiver had visited places that I would never dream of seeing. He presented it as a curiosity or a broader education of sorts. But it was clear that it was within this environment where his appetite for knowledge was most passionately rooted. That was unsettling. I mean, what type of faith-driven individual would seek to replicate death through a ritualistic experience?

In anticipation of the grand reveal of evil, we began having some very uncomfortable conversations regarding eternal salvation. His contention was that everyone was eligible, including those who committed the most heinous crimes against humanity in the natural world. Even though that made me extremely uneasy, my faith would not allow me to sit in the seat of judgment. Although I did not agree with him, I did believe that God could offer salvation to anyone that He chose. If a murderer, for example, repented and fell at the feet of Jesus Christ, who was I to say that the Savior would not offer that individual salvation? That was a decision well above my pay grade. I knew the love of the Father and the Son, and I thought, perhaps anything was possible. How could we as humans fully perceive the depth of God's mercy and grace?

That being said, I had a very difficult time accepting the idea that those who had raped, killed, or severely harmed children would ever find a simple road to salvation. My desire for such offenders was justice only. That became a major point of contention in our relationship. My deceiver repeatedly used this most twisted segment of society to turn the knife inside of me, continually reminding me that God loved them, too. He would direct me to "forgive them for they know not what they do." I had a very hard time with that.

I knew in my heart that many of those individuals knew exactly what they were doing. Most were acting without any remorse whatsoever.

As for their salvation, my deceiver once declared that he personally would act as their guide. He felt well conditioned to handle the darkness, so when the world awakened to the depth of their actions, he would be their leader. A brave mission perhaps, but one that I had no interest in serving. He was clear about the fact that it was not for me anyway. He took pride in the notion that only he was equipped to do that type of work. Ironic, right?

Following the courtship and our initial "healing" session together, there was a brief period when my deceiver drew back from consistent communication with me. Initially, he presented his "absence" as a period of planned solitude, rest, and spiritual renewal. Later, I exposed the false nature of that claim.

The move had been coordinated with thoughtful intention. He knew that once his seed was planted, his absence would create a longing. So he left in order that I might feel emptiness and confusion regarding how to step forward in my faith journey without him. Keep in mind the devil's end game: reverent submission. It's a carefully crafted scheme that involves patiently waiting for the follower to progress into the next level of captivity. Every step is calculated.

So when my deceiver reemerged from his absence, it was no coincidence that he immediately shared with me his desire to disappear once more, perhaps for months until the time when his followers were better prepared to receive his message. He had created the initial separation only to drop back in momentarily and threaten to leave once again. What he was seeking was my validation and buy-in. And that's exactly what he received.

"Stay here," I urged as I assumed the role of spiritual mentor, reinforcing my belief that we were "on a collective mission together." I felt moved to minister to him in the manner that he had taught me, and he loved it. In fact, I remember that he was repeatedly encouraging me to step into my power. I felt emboldened by that, so I missed the setup. He was allowing me to feel gifted so that I would embrace the idea that I had the ability to do what others could not. He was seeking loyalty by preying on my ego in a very manipulative manner.

You see, outside of my own unfolding story of deception, there were several others like me who were also involved in his courtship. My soul was not his only target. Not by a long shot. He was making every effort to build what he referred to as "the alliance." The trouble was that within any community my deceiver led, there was always dissention found rising in the ranks. He repeatedly claimed that to be the result of his followers' inability to go deeper, contending that his spirituality rose beyond the reach of others' capacity to understand.

Now he was telling me, "You get it." A deliberate ego stroke to lead me into a more committed, blind following of his ever-changing false doctrine. A doctrine that he would ultimately encourage me to use to deceive a legion of loyal followers among my Christian brethren.

When I "ministered" to my deceiver in his threat to go dark, he took notes. Every ounce of wisdom I shared with him was tactfully used as research into my heart intention and the current state of my spiritual mindset. He didn't have the ability to telepathically access my thoughts, so he needed me to lay the blueprint for the next phase of his deception. With that blueprint in hand, he drafted a new approach. It was one that was a bit less extreme and battle-oriented than what he had led with initially. With my buy-in, he appeared ready to move me on to the next evolution of his false doctrine. It was one that looked absolutely nothing like the first.

I began to notice dramatic changes in both the philosophy and actions of my deceiver, and that made me very uneasy. His tone became much softer than ever before. At one point, I remember reminding him that it was his boldness that had attracted me to his message. I urged him not to water down his truth. He contended that not everyone was ready for that. So he was going to begin scaling it back, restraining his most passionate energy for "masters" like me, again reinforcing that his broader message required mass appeal. That was the only path to the development of an "alliance."

Almost overnight, his religion became rooted in his interest in reconciling with the Divine Feminine. For the first time in our relationship, he began sharing with me his immersion in the practices of yoga and qigong. The idea of balance (yin and yang) started to dominate his conversation. No extremes. No good. No evil. Just oneness. Everything is God's creation. Love them all; this was the Christ consciousness as he would call it.

In Hinduism, the Divine Feminine is also known as Kundalini. Kundalini is the serpent energy thought to rest coiled up at the base of the spine in every human being. You may have heard people speak of a Kundalini awakening. This awakening is thought to lead to the ultimate state of spiritual enlightenment in which a person becomes aware and at one with the heavenly dimensions of the universe. It's extraordinarily dangerous. It's counter to the Christian faith. A major red flag.

Yet, despite my deceiver's knowledge of my faith's condemnation of such practices, he began sharing his budding appetite for awakening the Kundalini quite loosely. In doing so, he neglected to recall his previously spoken words from earlier in our courtship. He had initially stated that his religion was syncretic in nature (a blend), and although he believed in Jesus, Buddha, Mohammed, and so forth, Hinduism was a completely separate and obscure type of religion altogether, and it was one that he did not incorporate into his belief system. Now, hardly a day could pass without him leaving me a reminder of the Divine Feminine.

This radical adaptation of religion led me to recognize a number of things. Most importantly, I came to understand the chameleon-like nature of Satan. In the Garden of Eden, the devil presented himself as a snake. That's exactly the type of venomous role that he assumed in his manifestation to me, a spineless serpent energy floating false promises of spiritual transcendence and oneness with God. He was the embodiment of the shifting shadows. His "truth" was always a deception, carefully crafted to manipulate whichever prey he had lined in his sights. I was shocked by how erratic he could be with his message after spending years studying and training to arrive at his supposed God-given mission. This was not a reflection of my God. The God that I knew was consistent.

In time, I began connecting the dots to reveal the disparity between the new "religion" that he had chosen to embody and the initial deception that he had used to bait and hook me. The devil was aware of the destination that he was planning to guide me to all along. He simply advertised what he believed I would be willing to tolerate until the moment he received my buy-in or my willingness to draw deeper into reliance on him and his twisted "faith." Then he would seek my soul.

CHAPTER 18

THE BAD FRUIT

THE ASCENDED MASTER
OF THE NEW AGE

He replied: "Watch out that you are not deceived. For many will come in my name, claiming, 'I am he,' and, 'The time is near.' Do not follow them." (Luke 21:8)

THE IDEA OF REINCARNATION AND THE "OLD SOUL" became a major uniting force solidifying the bond between me and my deceiver throughout the duration of our second encounter. He taught me to believe that our souls had been uniquely prepared for the missions that we were being called to serve in this most critical period of humanity. He often told me, "There weren't many like us." That made me feel special. We were divinely chosen and equipped to fulfill the master plan of God.

The warning of the appearance of false prophets is presented countless times throughout the Bible. To that notion, I was completely tuned out. I had zero understanding of the Ascended Master Teachings of the New Age religion. For the duration of our second courtship, I remained oblivious. My deceiver intentionally hid the inner workings of his master plan and disguised any aspects that he did reveal to me in such a way that they appeared to be of no threat to my established Christian beliefs.

He was very clear about recognizing Jesus as an Ascended Master. In the New Age teachings, that's a commonly accepted fact. Mother Mary also receives that designation along with Buddha. The idea is that these Ascended Masters have evolved, abandoning any differences that they may have experienced in the natural world to support humanity as a whole in its collective spiritual journey. This was the philosophy that motivated my former mentor to encourage me to "look for the commonalities" as we were all in the journey together in pursuit of "The One" God, or the Universal All-Pervading Presence of Life.

As I began to recognize the diverging nature of our beliefs regarding the pathway to God and eternal salvation, I reaffirmed repeatedly my belief that Jesus was the one and only Judge. I also accepted the fact that not everyone knew Jesus. In some parts of the world, there remains no knowledge of His ministry. Was Jesus going to deny those who never had access to Him salvation if they fell at His feet and accepted

Him as their Lord and Savior on the day of reckoning? Perhaps. That was another decision outside of my pay grade. I did recognize the possibility that there may be multiple paths to Him. But I remained committed to my belief that Jesus Christ would have the final say regarding the salvation of every soul.

At varying times throughout our second encounter, my deceiver would refer to me as Master Matt. He enjoyed defining this separation of our pact from the rest of society. That felt good to me. Ironically, it fueled my ego, the very thing that I had openly professed to be killing off. He also offered me the nickname The Apostle. This was another tactful hook deliberately chosen to appease my Christian faith. He was careful to present constant subtle reassurances to help me feel that we were never deviating from my known and accepted Truth. In my ignorance, I embraced them all.

The devil's shadows were always shifting. This was extraordinarily evident in his recognition and acknowledgment of Jesus. At the onset of our second meeting with each other, my deceiver identified Jesus as "an avatar" placing Him on the same level as Mohammed and Buddha. But in order to not reduce the figurehead of my faith to a level that would cause me concern, he also mentioned that he had allowed Jesus into his own personal faith journey. He claimed that Yeshua was one of his spirit guides, going so far as to say that he even "walked" with Him. Admittedly, that did give me some comfort.

That comfort was further advanced by stories he would share from healers who did work on him and reportedly witnessed Jesus in his presence. He once even had a woman approach him and claim that he was the second coming of Christ. He told me that for a moment, he believed it before returning to his senses.

I began to notice, however, that his behavior rarely reflected what I believed to be the Light of Christ. He was often angry and resentful to those who did not openly submit to his message and will. His tongue was frequently disturbingly perverse. Perverse not only as it related to his conquests among females, but also with regard to spirituality. He would often use sexual perversion to state things to me about the wake-up call that God was going to give me in my faith journey, or to describe the liberal sexual awakening that I would experience via the work of the Hand of God. He used slang terminology so perverse that in my ignorance, I couldn't even recognize it as being sexual. I'd simply laugh it off in the moment, and then later, I'd research the term online to reveal the meaning. I'd find myself sickened by its repulsive nature.

Was this someone who really knew and walked with Jesus? MY Jesus? Or was this simply his crude and corrupt interpretation? Where was the real Jesus being lost? Was it in this idea of the Ascended Master?

As we approached the breaking point in our relationship, my deceiver began encouraging me to set the Bible aside. Anticipating my resistance to this radical proposed step in my faith journey, he would repeatedly say, "I'm not telling you to get rid of it," but you should first "allow yourself to get to know the teacher, and then the teachings will make more sense to you." Part of that theory made sense to me. More depth would be revealed in the teachings with a greater understanding of the Man Himself. Sure. But I had a real issue with setting the Bible aside. Thankfully, I never did. Because that Bible was my primary representation of the Truth.

So who was this Ascended Master Jesus? The only way I would ever find out was by allowing a spiritual guide on an equal level of enlightenment to make an introduction for me. At least that's what my deceiver wanted me to believe. So perhaps that's why in the final days, he came to me and shared that he had arrived at the conclusion that he, too, was an Ascended Master who had descended to accept his calling to awaken souls like my own. I personally could never become an Ascended Master; he was very clear about that. But he, on the other hand, embodied a soul that had navigated the complexities of a journey through centuries upon centuries in the natural world, preparing him for the moment in time when he would act as a critical piece of the spiritual unification that would ultimately unfold.

Now, if you think that sounds crazy, let me warn you, it gets worse. At one point near the end of our relationship with each other, we were having a conversation live, and I made a comment related to being the likeness of Jesus. I openly stated that "I would NEVER say that I am Jesus" but that I was comfortable stating that "the blood of Jesus" flows through me. Later in that same conversation (interestingly as I was reaffirming my commitment to my journey in Christ), he made a comment that made me shudder. In a very matter-of-fact tone, my deceiver said to me, "I am Jesus." He argued that I should trust him because he could not possibly deviate from the path of Christ since Christ was in him. He explained his statement by claiming to me that he held "a fragment of Jesus's soul" inside of himself.

These statements had elevated the threat of the false doctrine to a completely different level. Within a short time frame, we had transitioned from "Jesus is an avatar" to "Jesus is one of my spirit guides" to "I reflect the Christ consciousness" to "I am an Ascended Master," essentially on the same level as Jesus, to "I am Jesus because I embody a fragment of His soul," and I cannot possibly deceive or mislead you (even if I tried) because "I am Him." Wow. Talk about going all in. It seemed that the longer that I resisted my deceiver's advances, the more brash his efforts became. He was not going to stop until he had me, even if it meant proclaiming boldly that he himself was Jesus Christ.

CHAPTER 19

THE BAD FRUIT

MONISM, PANTHEISM, AND RELATIVISM

See to it that no one takes you captive through hollow and deceptive philosophy, which depends on human tradition and the elemental spiritual forces of this world rather than on Christ. For in Christ all the fullness of the Deity lives in bodily form, and in Christ you have been brought to fullness. He is the head over every power and authority. (Colossians 2:8–10)

THE PHILOSOPHIES OF NEW AGE RELIGION AND enlightenment are extraordinarily complex. Earlier in the book, I described the work of the devil as the web of a spider. Every morning, the spider weaves an intricate deceitful scheme for his prey. This, too, is the nature of the evil one. He relentlessly shapes his wide-reaching webs to capture believers in the grips of false religions, philosophies, and deities that are in opposition to the Father and His one and only Son Jesus Christ.

Within the intricate teachings and principles of the New Age religion, the devil finds great security. It's a comfortable place to stalk his prey and recruit new followers. Inside of it, there exist foundational beliefs that in some cases extend to other more broadly established religions of the world, such as Hinduism. For the purpose of this chapter, I am going to focus on three: monism, pantheism, and relativism. I will speak to each of them not as a subject matter expert but rather as a novice observer. What truly matters is not the beliefs themselves but rather how the devil attempts to lure us away from God using these principles.

Let's start with monism. The philosophy is essentially that we all originate from the same source, and to the same source we will all eventually return. In my second encounter with my deceiver, he led his message with the idea of a collective ascension to the God that he called "The One." The unification of the Ascended Masters was evidence of the steps needed to bring salvation to all through the creation and teaching of a path to oneness with God.

My deceiver often spoke in terms of mirroring with relation to this collective oneness. If, for instance, my wife was experiencing hesitancy or angst in my presence, it was only a reflection of my own resistance or inner turmoil. So in a sense, if I shifted my energy, I could shift my perception of hers as well. Since all of God's life-forms derived from one source, this practice could be used anywhere. Essentially, it provided an individual the power to control his or her own surroundings. Very literally, it allowed you to become the god of your own life, the most rotten sin at the root of Lucifer's downfall. In my own sinful nature, I had yearned for control throughout my life. So sadly, I offered very little opposition to this philosophy. Instead, I went deeper.

Within the oneness, I came to feel my arms wrapping around humanity with one giant collective hug. In many ways, that was not a bad thing at all. For we know that Scripture teaches us that "love covers over a multitude of sins" (1 Peter 4:8). Love everyone. Let God be the Judge. That felt pure. I embraced that doctrine wholeheartedly and thought, maybe this oneness idea isn't such a bad thing.

Then, in walked pantheism and relativism, two principles that really challenged the core foundation of my faith. Pantheism essentially means that all is God. Relativism is the notion that since God is all things, we must also conclude that God is present in things that humanity defines both as good and as evil. That's where it gets really ugly. No line between good and evil? Nope. Those distinctions are simply the illusions of humanity. Being that they are an illusion, then ignorance is the primary issue of man and woman and enlightenment is the most plausible solution.

My deceiver had me at monism. I was filled with love for humanity, and I'll admit, I enjoyed playing God, so I was too blind to see the nature of my most tragic sin. But the idea of attaching God to the morally corrupt creations of humanity and the things of the world that were out of line with His Perfect Intention gave me pause. I could not view something that was clearly evil and say that God's Hands were in it. I knew the perfect love of my Father in Heaven and His Son Jesus Christ, and in that love, there was not an ounce of evil at all. For me to assign that label to God, I felt that I would be committing the most devastating betrayal of my life. I would be choosing the devil over the Truth. That was not a decision I wanted to make.

My deceiver cleverly walked me into this trap, seeking my buy-in at every phase. First, he allowed me to embrace the warmth of his false light. That led me to this feeling of oneness both in our relationship and also in my own personal relationships that extended beyond him. That oneness filled my heart with love and led me to a seemingly pure desire to spread my message of joy and hope to all things because essentially, all things were me and all things were God.

As that love began to wash over me, Satan started to reveal his scheme and the true reality of his doctrine. If your desire is to love all things made in the image of God, then you better choose to love evil, too. Because within the dark corners of society, in those heinous crimes against humanity,

God is there also and so are you. There really is no such thing as evil. I know you believe that you were sent here to serve a mission in opposition to it, but that was just an illusion. In fact, that's the downfall of humanity. We perpetuate our suffering through the division. The key is balance.

Balance. No absolute good. No absolute evil. Morality is subjective. Therefore, so is sin. Throw out God's rule book. You define your values. Through enlightenment, you are the god of your life. In collective ascension, we will rebuild God's Kingdom on earth. We will create Heaven as though it is ours to give.

The devil never outlined his philosophy this way. If he had, I would have turned and ran. Instead, he fed me bits and pieces as he led me deeper into his web of lies. At times, I was overwhelmed with confusion. But I was always taking inventory of my surroundings. Piece by piece, I accumulated the evidence I needed to reveal the motives of his underlying vicious scheme.

CHAPTER 20

THE BAD FRUIT

FALSE "LIGHT"

And no wonder, for Satan himself masquerades as an angel of
light. It is not surprising, then, if his servants also masquerade
as servants of righteousness. Their end will be what their actions
deserve. (2 Corinthians 11:14–15)

MY DECEIVER WAS A FAST TALKER. AS I MENTIONED
several times previously, he was highly intelligent. It was
difficult to challenge him because his depth of knowledge
(hint: awareness) was beyond the reach of any other being
that I had encountered throughout my life. The wisdom
that he shared often rushed over me like a flood. I felt overwhelmed in my efforts to process it. My mind was always
racing to catch up. I never had the opportunity to stop,
absorb it all, and ask more of the pressing questions that I
should have been asking.

In response to any questions that I did ask, I frequently received very complex responses. I'll be honest, I was a bit intimidated by his intellectual superiority, so even when things remained unclear, I often felt afraid to pry deeper or offer a rebuttal. In the rare moments when I would speak counter to his truth, he would interrupt me before I could vocalize the point that I had intended to make. So I never received any real peace of mind about the areas of his spirituality that were trouble spots for me.

What's interesting is that in the midst of all of the fast talk, my deceiver would often caution me to pace myself. Those words were not sincere, of course. They were chosen deliberately as fuel for my ego. It was this notion that I had the capacity to absorb a greater depth of knowledge than others in a more accelerated fashion than most could ever process. He would frequently tell me, "You are up-leveling quickly" and "You've done a lot in a short period of time." But he never stopped reminding me of my need to rely on him for my future path to enlightenment.

Knowledge was everything to my deceiver. He wanted me to understand that I had not come close to achieving the level of wisdom required to lead. In his eyes, my Truth was rooted in ignorance. I shouldn't be so bold as to share the teachings of my teacher (Jesus Christ) until I actually met the teacher Himself. Put the Bible on the shelf and revisit it later when you are equipped to decipher it properly. Don't spew your ignorance. You'll just have to walk it back later. Wait until you have MY corrupt teachings embedded in your soul, then speak. I'll tell you when you are ready.

Amid the chaos of the flood of baseless knowledge overwhelming my soul, there was a subtle nudge that I could not ignore. It was the Word of God. It had taken root in me over many years of study, and it was finally beginning to bloom in the midst of the greatest spiritual battle of my life. The Word caused my stomach to churn on the new deceptive wisdom that was being introduced to displace my Truth. It inspired me to dig deeper to reveal the enemy. The resounding message remained, "You will know them by their fruit." I could feel God imploring me to slow down, to process the deceit, and begin to more deeply acknowledge the red flags that I had witnessed.

My deceiver was well aware of this threat. That's why he spoke quickly and attempted to overwhelm me with his knowledge. If he could keep me chasing his perverse doctrine, he could steer my focus away from the stillness and firmness of God's Truth. He knew that the Bible's teachings would lead to his downfall if I did not choose to surrender them. Ironically, the greatest threat to his awareness-driven motives was my own awareness.

I once heard a statistic referenced in a sermon that concluded only six in ten people believe that the devil exists. To me, that is shockingly low. Perhaps fear is causing denial among many believers in God. I'm not sure. What I can tell you is that the devil is, in fact, very real. Personally, I'd much rather be aware of my enemy so I can identify and resist him rather than pretend he doesn't exist and be caught like a sitting duck when he makes his advance.

Ironically, it was awareness disguised as "the Light of God" that led me into the grips of the evil one's grand deception. To my deceiver, awareness was the light, which served as the key ingredient for spiritual transformation. Of course, that was not the way it was presented during the early stages of our courtship. The devil allowed me to believe that my Light aligned with his light. My Light being the Light of God, Jesus Christ, the Holy Spirit.

I, too, believed that the Light of God was the key ingredient in spiritual transformation. After all, God had used His Perfect Light to expose what was dark in my life and lead me to my own spiritual rebirth. I believed He would do the same for others as well. God would bring into the Light any hidden evils so His righteous judgment and pure love could shine. His Light would cause conviction among sinners and evildoers and demand repentance. In time, that repentance would lead to the transformation and salvation of many previously lost souls.

I was ready to go all in to magnify the Light of God. I

believed this would be the most critical element for surviving the onslaught of darkness that was sure to overwhelm humanity in the near future. I dived in with blind disregard, never pausing to first qualify the nature of the light that was leading me. I simply moved in the faithful expectation that anything grounded in the light had to be pure. I lost sight of the teaching that I needed most: "Satan himself masquerades as an angel of light."

In doing a little quick research on the fallen angel Lucifer, you can quickly uncover that his very name means "light bringer." Lucifer was once a magnificent being who was created in the Likeness of God. At some point, he rebelled against God out of his prideful heart, and as a result, he was cast out of Heaven for eternity. He apparently was so obsessed with his own beauty, intelligence, and power that he sought to essentially replace God by defying Him through his own free will. This free will became the origin of sin prior to the formation of man and woman.

When God created man and woman, Lucifer was present as the serpent in the Garden of Eden. In the garden, he tempted Eve and led her to taste the forbidden fruit of the Tree of the Knowledge of Good and Evil (remember light = awareness by Luciferian standards), creating humanity's enslavement to sin until the moment when Jesus Christ gave His blood as an atonement, allowing us to achieve eternal salvation despite our sinful nature. Lucifer wanted to play

God, and in choosing that fate, he became God's adversary or Satan. The Satan of the garden is the very same Satan that we, the children of God, are at war with today.

In seeking his prey, the evil one leads with the very same Luciferian temptations that cast him out of Heaven before we ever walked God's green earth. Those temptations are rooted in a false light or awareness. By the devil's standards, evil is not intended to be exposed for the purpose of judgment and repentance but rather for enlightenment. The message he portrays is that it is through the awareness of all things good and evil and an elevated state of consciousness (and supposed ascension) that we will achieve oneness with God. In ascension, we are said to achieve the perfect balance of blended energy. Good and evil are simply illusory designations assigned by man. In reality, there is no good or evil. Morality is subjective. In collective harmony, we become our own gods.

This is quite a convenient story for the fallen angel who rebelled against God and was cast out of Heaven for eternity. Broken, cowardly, and supremely egotistic, the devil has continued actively seeking to play God in our worldly plane. He misleads Truth seekers with a false light and the idea that Heaven can be created on earth through greater access to knowledge. It is an endearing story for those seeking to avoid conviction and repentance.

Think for a moment about the frightening nature of a

world where "the light" of knowledge made us aware of all things, even things that were rooted in darkness beyond our human comprehension. In the awareness, the darkness was assigned no label. No condemnation. No judgment. No consequences. All of the devil's works would essentially go unnoticed. We would be asked to accept that God's Hands have been in every single one of the most heinous crimes ever to occur on this earth. Acts that were committed not by God but by the hands of sinful men and women who have been rebelling against God through the temptations of Satan since the very beginning of time. That's not Heaven. That is Hell.

This world is the devil's playground. It will never EVER be Heaven. Heaven awaits those who persevere and stay committed to the Truth in the Word of God. It awaits those who repent of their sins and seek their salvation through the grace and mercy of our Lord Jesus Christ, who died on the cross to ensure that we may have an opportunity to receive a different fate than that of Lucifer. Any religion, philosophy, or practice that disregards the need for repentance and forgiveness of sin as the defining factor in eternal salvation is the work of the devil. I can tell you that with confidence because I met him personally, and I understand the nature of the lies that he is selling.

So when you speak of the Light, make sure your light aligns with the light of the eternal community that you are seeking.

Otherwise, you may find that you have been deceptively led down a path that offers a far different fate than the one that is offered through the blood of our Lord, Jesus Christ. A fate where there is no light present at all, only eternal darkness.

The devil is very real and he is not easy to spot. Much of what he uses against us can feel quite familiar, and in that familiarity, there often arises a natural presumption of security. Why would anyone fear the light? For me, light over darkness was a concept that was very compatible with my faith. The evil one recognized this. You can trust that he understands the Bible's teachings very well. He is an adversary who is absolutely OBSESSED with knowledge. Knowledge is his basis for manipulation. His goal is to pervert the Word of God and lead believers astray with a false doctrine and an evil imposter that appears (at least initially) to align with and complement principles of our known and established Truth. It's when he has your commitment that his true motives become clear. You begin to see the divergence between his false light and its accompanying philosophies and the real Light of God.

CHAPTER 21

MYSTICAL SUBMISSION

Let no one be found among you who sacrifices their son or daughter in the fire, who practices divination or sorcery, interprets omens, engages in witchcraft, or casts spells, or who is a medium or spiritist or who consults the dead. (Deuteronomy 18:10–11)

MY RELATIONSHIP WITH GOD AS A YOUTH WAS BASIcally nonexistent. As I mentioned earlier, I was baptized in a very traditional Lutheran church, and I attended Sunday school and worship services with my family on a regular basis. But I was tuned out. There was nothing about my religion that led me to feel closer to God. So when I stepped out into the real world, my faith foundation was extraordinarily weak and vulnerable. I believed in God. I believed in Heaven. But I really took no interest in caring for my soul. I was living for the now. Eternity was an afterthought.

When I finally did reconnect with my Creator in 2011, it was a completely different faith experience than anything I had ever encountered before. Jesus sought me, and I invited Him into my life. I began absorbing the Word, and the Truth tugged at my heart and convicted me. I repented, and He purified me and made me new. As my faith strengthened, I witnessed miracles unfold in my life that were undoubtedly the work of His hands. God pulled me out of a pit of darkness that no human could possibly navigate in their own strength.

In the midst of my divine intervention, I finally allowed myself to feel the pure love of my Father in Heaven. From the moment of my very first breath, He had loved me unconditionally. For many years, I never gave Him a thing in return. I was too busy in my rebellion to stop and pay Him any attention. I really didn't know Him, so it wasn't in my nature to seek His love and compassion. And it certainly wasn't in my nature to believe in His miraculous power or to follow His Will for my life. So when He showed up in my life, His presence literally turned my world upside down. Through my experiences, I began to understand who He was, and I quickly developed a completely different view of the Christian faith altogether. It was as if everything had finally clicked for me.

I discovered God in the solitude of agoraphobia. He ministered to me when no one else could find the words to comfort my sorrows. He gave me hope when there was none to be found in the world around me. It was clear I didn't need a church to find Jesus. I simply needed the Word and an earnest appetite for the Truth. To build my relationship with Him, I simply needed to pray, to listen, and then direct my steps forward according to His Will. By doing those few things, I'd begin to witness His miracles in my life.

Miracles became a focal point of my growing faith. I expected them because I lived them. So I began to seek them in everything I encountered throughout my day. Nothing was a coincidence. Everything had meaning. I recognized that God was always working. He was always present in my life. I intended to give Him the glory whenever I found myself on an easy road and to seek His wisdom and guidance whenever the path grew bumpy. This, I believed, was His Will.

There were things about the church that continued to leave me feeling dissatisfied, just as they had in my youth. I wanted to go deeper with Christ. I wanted to know Him on a more intimate level. I wanted to feel the Holy Spirit guiding me. I recognized its power, and I fully understood the emptiness I felt when I was led by my own desires. I never really believed the church could deliver that relationship to me. So I sought to create the intimacy on my own.

When my deceiver arrived in my life for the second time, one of the things that appealed to me about him was his appetite for mysticism. For years, I had wanted to know Jesus on a more intimate level. Now perhaps I had uncovered the way. Maybe I simply needed someone to light the path for me?

Over time, as I drew nearer to my deceiver, I also drew nearer to the surreal. I learned to anticipate it daily. He had taught me to understand that unexplainable things would begin to happen in my life with great frequency as my faith was more fully activated. I believed that the mystical cues I was receiving were the work of God and the result of an emboldened Holy Spirit within me. So I grew quite enamored by them as they began presenting themselves to me. I trusted they were sent to me with intention, and I sought to use them to direct my steps forward. I actually became a bit of a rookie shaman. I began to substitute my experiences with the surreal for direct conversation with God in prayer.

I was playing with fire. I was completely unaware of the threat. In Revelation chapter 13, we read about the beast of the earth and the "great signs" that he will be able to perform to deceive the earth's people. I knew the warnings of dabbling in the occult, but I wanted to believe that my growing appetite for mysticism was innocent and that I was completely protected from the schemes of the evil one because my heart was purely rooted in faith.

Then the day arrived of my great deception. It was just before dawn on the morning of my forty-first day in the wilderness.

I was driving to the park where I had been devoting my mornings to solitude for prayer and reflection with God. As I neared my destination, I sensed something powerful coming over me. I was wide awake, but I began to feel as though I was being led into a dreamlike state. It felt a bit like an out-of-body experience. A little unsettling, but I thought it had to be the Holy Spirit preparing to reveal something of great significance to me.

I remember that I repeatedly experienced nausea whenever another car would pass by me on the road. Now, keep in mind, this was a very quiet period of the day. The sun had not yet even risen in the sky. There was very little traffic to be found. On this particular morning, however, the presence of even one car was too many. Everything of the world that man had created felt to me like noise or interference that I needed to somehow drown out of my mind and my heart. I yearned to detach and create a space for stillness in that moment.

When I arrived at the park, I pulled into the lot and discovered I was in fact alone. As I left the car, I had this sense that running may not be in the cards for me. I trusted that the feelings overcoming me were God's presence, and what I believed was that He was telling me to slow down and allow. I decided to test the run to be sure, and I went maybe fifty to one hundred yards and then stopped. I had the confirmation I was seeking. No run. Just listen. This day was going to be different.

Moments later, I felt my eyes drawn to the sky. I saw a cloud that appeared to be in the shape of a cross. So I pulled out my phone and snapped a photo and then proceeded to record a three-and-a-half-minute video to document my experiences to that point. This was at 6:30 a.m. I summarized much of what I was feeling in that state and then concluded the video with one final message that had been placed in my heart, and that was to "go somewhere meaningful to you and pray."

At that point, I began seeking the surreal. I had this anticipation that God was going to show me something. My senses were finely tuned, awaiting His cues. About a quarter of a mile down the path, I paused at a set of trees where I would often witness the radiant sun shining through as it rose above the horizon. I would frequently capture photos there on my phone as I ran on by. The setting felt so majestic to me. It always made me feel connected to my Creator. So naturally, I concluded it would be the ideal spot for me to "go and pray."

When I arrived, my eyes were again drawn back to the sky. My heart felt connected to the cloud that had formed in the shape of a cross moments earlier, and I was anticipating that the sun may light the world in a divine fashion on this day. It did not disappoint. It was an overcast morning, but what I witnessed was this perfect break in the clouds that allowed for the rising sun's light to shine through in brilliant fashion. To me, it appeared to resemble a stairway to Heaven. As I stopped to pray, I asked God if it would be okay if I allowed my eyes to remain open. It was so magical. I didn't want to miss a thing.

As I stood and watched, I noticed that at the base of the stairway, there was a gate that was slowly beginning to close. The gate arrived in the form of a lower lying cloud formation that was moving into the plane. It was almost like a fog. To me, it appeared to be a veil of sorts. It soon covered my access point to this stairway. As I finished praying and continued moving along the path, I felt further into the visual phenomenon that I had just experienced. My contention was that my journey was offering me a glimpse of God's majesty but that there remained something clouding my view. There was a veil that needed to be removed.

I continued walking about another fifty yards before I stopped to observe a rabbit that had appeared along the path. I recalled that I would often see this particular rabbit at the very same spot and at the same time each morning. It was as if we had a breakfast date scheduled with each other.

On this morning, I paused to watch him eat, and I chuckled to myself and said out loud, "God will provide." The rabbit didn't worry about what he would find in the pantry each morning. When the new day arrived, he stepped out of the forest knowing that God would care for his needs. Every morning, I witnessed His miracle unfold right in front of me. "God will provide," I repeated. How beautiful.

From that spot, I walked just a short distance before my eyes were drawn to a pond on my right-hand side where a number of plants were growing. I noticed these beautiful, brilliant white flowers reaching toward the sky along the edge. I felt moved to take a closer look at them. So I walked over and captured a couple of photos with my phone. What struck me was that these particular flowers (Luna White Hibiscus) had such amazingly pure white petals with a sort of bleeding-heart center. It reminded me of the purity and blood of Jesus Christ and His amazing sacrifice. Another sign, I thought.

Farther down, I approached a canopy of trees. As I drew nearer, I began to again grow overwhelmed by nausea as I reflected on the world around me. The things that man had created in this world were dead and decaying. I started to acknowledge in that moment that the only places where I felt at peace were within God's untouched creation—the grass, the trees, the sunlight, and so on. I was at home within the things He had made out of His pure intention. Among the world created by man, I felt detached. To me, while those structures remained present in the natural, they were essentially dead because they were not created in the Likeness of God. I was beginning to conclude that I could not exist in that world any longer.

As I pondered my existence, the yearning that overcame me upon entering the canopy of trees was profound. I knew beyond a doubt that I wanted to go deeper with Jesus Christ. I felt that I needed to better understand His mysticism because I was no longer of this world. There wasn't a place for me here, I thought. In that moment, as I accepted those feelings as my truth, I began to feel as though I was detaching from my body once again. It was as if I was stepping back into a dreamlike state. I felt as though I was floating and like I was walking into an alternative dimension with God.

Emerging from the canopy, a message came to me regarding my deceiver. It was time for me to draw nearer to him. I was ready to make a financial commitment toward my training. The message had arrived with perfect clarity. The number, which I had never sought to attempt to define previously, became crystal clear.

I concluded that what had been holding me back from making this decision sooner was my old conditioning. I was afraid to let go. The snares of dogma had kept me captive. With God sending me all of these signals and placing the vision into my heart, how could I deny the path forward now? Perhaps my commitment was in fact the veil that needed to be lifted in order for me to see the complete stairway to Heaven.

As I allowed this vision to take root in me, I began to think more about the financial obligation of advanced training. Did it make sense? Was this a smart risk? I needed another sign to put my mind at ease. Moments later, as I glanced to my left, I noticed another rabbit sitting next to me on the path. I could have almost stepped on him. He was looking up at me, and I took his appearance as the signal that "God will provide," as I breathed a sigh of relief in reassurance.

The signs were everywhere. In no way did I anticipate drawing the conclusion that I made that morning at all. I had been feeling more and more that I was going to tackle my spiritual journey all on my own. Then, like a ton of bricks, these events hit me. That led me to believe they had to have been aligned by God because they really weren't my will. So they had to be His. I was ready to step forward in faith and embrace that call. I wanted to peel back the layers so I could see and get to know Jesus on a more intimate level.

"Allow" was a popular term presented throughout my deception. Submission is always the end goal of the deceiver. He makes his push systematically. Step by step, he seeks to weaken you until you are prone to fall victim to his advances. My desire to connect with the mystical nature of my faith had been established over many years. This was an area where I was vulnerable. The devil is an opportunist. Wherever there is a crack in the foundation, he will find a way to weasel his way in and take root. That's exactly how he cornered me.

I felt that in order to live my faith, I had no other choice than to trust the signals. I had to allow. The issue was that it wasn't God making the play calls. It was an imposter from the opposing sideline. His will was not to draw me nearer in relationship with Jesus but to ensure that I would never know the real Christ ever again.

CHAPTER 22

UNMASKING THE DEVIL

Put on the full armor of God, so that you can take your stand
against the devil's schemes. For our struggle is not against flesh
and blood, but against the rulers, against the authorities, against
the powers of this dark world and against the spiritual forces
of evil in the heavenly realms. (Ephesians 6:11–12)

BEYOND THE LEGACY THAT I INTEND TO LEAVE BEHIND
for my own children, my primary motivation for writing this
book is to glorify God by providing all of His children with
the framework to understand the work of the evil one. For
the vast majority of my life, I was ill-prepared to turn away
the advances of the devil. From the days of my childhood
leading up to the point of my nervous breakdown and my
eventual rebirth in faith, I was a puppet for the prince of
darkness. The devil governed my thought life. He moved

me to take action according to the desires of my flesh. That led to devastating consequences. I was completely oblivious to any outside spiritual influence whatsoever. My lack of understanding of the Truth made me an easy target. The fact of the matter was that there was no real way for me to identify the presence of evil in my life if I wasn't first grounded in my own relationship with God.

I had the opportunity to unmask the devil in our first encounter, but I chose not to listen to the Holy Spirit's warning. I knew beyond a doubt that what I was confronting was pure evil, and I went forward anyway. I was blinded by my desire for money and power, and I did not care to see beyond my flesh. I basically looked God directly in the eyes and said, "I know better than you. Trust me on this one. I've got it." It was shameful. And it led to awful consequences that set me back several years in various areas of my life, most critically in my relationship with God.

By round two, I was far better prepared, or so I thought. My knowledge of the Word had certainly evolved, and I had become much less vulnerable to the desires of my flesh. My relationship with the Creator was stronger than it had been in quite some time. I was earnestly seeking the guidance of the Holy Spirit and working to align my mission with the Will of God. I was aware of many of the influences of evil in our society, and I had begun committing myself to become a voice of transformation. But the devil was progressing in his opposition to me as well. As I matured in faith, he silently observed and grew more intricate in his deception. The stakes were higher now than ever before. He wasn't going to hold back a thing.

Captivated by the mysticism of a false Jesus, I was getting closer to a commitment that had the potential to lead my soul into the captivity of darkness for eternity. I was on the verge of signing my life away yet again, and then the Lord intervened. I began to feel my stomach begin to churn over the path that I was getting ready to follow. Something just didn't seem right. Maybe I didn't need assistance with my spiritual transformation after all. Perhaps I should just continue navigating my faith journey on my own. I remembered that it was in solitude where I found an intimate connection with Jesus once before. Why couldn't I find Him there again?

In my angst, however, I remained quite captive to my desire to seek divine guidance through mystical cues. So as I reached the fork in the road in my relationship with my deceiver, I headed back out into the wilderness and began to prayerfully ask for direction. I went to a place very sacred to me and called out to the Lord, asking Him (vocally) to "show me if it's impure or let me feel into it if it's the Truth." In response to the word "impure," I heard a bird call several times. Then moments later, I felt a moth land on my left bicep. These events were quite unsettling. For the first time ever, noticeably dark cues were appearing in a place where I least expected them.

When I emerged from the trees, other signals arrived that appeared to be positive. I couldn't make sense of any of it. The experience really offered me no definitive direction. I began recognizing that I could not make this decision simply using mystical signals as my guide. There was no way for me to discern the God-inspired cues from those directed by evil. Overwhelmed with confusion, I stepped away and allowed some space for deeper reflection and prayer.

Time was critical. My deceiver had planned to go deeper with me immediately upon my commitment. But God created an opportunity for me to reflect. A conflict had arisen. I was given the window that I needed to reveal the deceit. He was going to lead me to the Truth. I just needed to be patient and listen.

For the first time in months, I was beginning to experience anxiety once again. Those feelings didn't appear to align with God's Will. I had been so clear and calm. Was this simply my fear of letting go of my old conditioning, or was I truly being deceived?

I thought back to my first encounter with the devil. I remembered the unsettling feeling I had experienced when the Holy Spirit revealed to me the evil nature of my deceiver. I told myself, you cannot allow this to happen again. This time, it was bigger than money. My soul was now on the line. This was serious business.

On the day of my resistance, I woke up with an odd and persistent question in my heart. What exactly was qigong? Would practicing qigong expose me to anything dark? You see, I was trying to understand what type of environment I may be subjecting myself to in leaning into a closer relationship with my deceiver. I knew very little about his advanced curriculum. So I started focusing on analyzing and diagnosing the nature of what I did know. I recalled him mentioning to me his desire to get me involved with qigong as soon as possible.

I did a little research into the practice, and I found that there were loads of conflicting information about it. You could find evidence to support any conclusion you were seeking. If you wanted to believe that it was harmless, there were plenty of resources to back that notion. If you wanted to uncover its dangers, there were countless testimonials revealing its dark side. I wasn't finding any clarity. The research was making my head feel like it was going to explode. There was no peace of mind, only an increasing belly churn and internal conflict. I paused on that subject momentarily, and I started down a different path.

My next question was, what type of works had been done

in the realm of Christian mysticism? Was this really a thing, or were my beliefs and pursuits entirely sinful in nature? I grappled with this as I recalled the words in Deuteronomy 18 regarding practices of the occult. Was I unknowingly committing sin by seeking signs from God? My actions didn't feel wrong because my intention truly was to be led by the Holy Spirit. But I began to wonder if it was wrong to have visions. Or to believe that God could light my path through His Creation. Again, I began to feel overcome with intensifying, stomach-churning nausea. Then I discovered Saint Teresa of Ávila.

I uncovered an article that referenced her work, and some of the quotes from pieces of her writing deeply resonated with me. I felt a powerful connection to her spiritually. I wanted to learn more about her. Initially, I was guided to a brief three-minute video overview of her life and her works on YouTube. At the very end of the video, the narrator stated that Saint Teresa's Feast Day was October 15. I got chills. October 15 was my birthday.

Teresa's work connected with me because it validated my belief that you can indeed seek and establish a more perfect soul union with Jesus Christ without heading down the path of witchcraft. As a nun, Christian mystic, and religious reformer, Teresa of Ávila, experienced powerful visions that inspired her writings. She was at the forefront of teaching contemplative prayer ("Devotion of the Heart"). Contemplative prayer was the first phase of a four-step process that she outlined for creating a pathway for the soul's ascent to God.

Teresa was deeply connected to Jesus Christ. She had vivid visions that led her to believe she was experiencing the presence of Christ in the physical. Those particular visions created a passion within her for imitating the life and suffering of Jesus all of the days of her life. Teresa was profoundly moved by the Holy Spirit, to the point that she would often levitate, particularly while taking communion during Catholic mass. Can you imagine witnessing that in church today?

Perhaps most important in all of this as it relates to my connection to her journey was that she acknowledged sin and the presence of evil. In fact, she wrote about a vision that God once gave her of Hell. It was an extremely unsettling account. Although the vision terrified her in the moment, she was deeply thankful for the fact that God had provided her with the experience. It taught her that no pain (of which she had quite a bit, particularly in her early life) that she would encounter in the flesh could ever compare to what a soul would endure in the depths of Hell. She was overwhelmed by God's mercy as her deliverer from the fiery flames. The vision inspired her to let go of fear and stand tall in a world that was in direct conflict with God.

I believed in Heaven and Hell. I believed in good and evil.

And I believed that God drew a line in the sand between the two. For me, there was no middle ground. So it was really encouraging to encounter a Christian mystic who embraced the real Jesus Christ, the one and only Son of God who offered Himself as a sacrifice for our sins so that our souls may have the opportunity to experience eternity with Him in Heaven. It was refreshing to encounter a mystic who understood Christ as a deliverer and not just an avatar or an Ascended Master who was part of a coalition of spiritual leaders responsible for leading souls to salvation through the creation of a false Heaven on earth.

Thanks to Saint Teresa of Ávila, I began to understand there was a different way to seek the mysticism of Christ and remain true to my core beliefs. I started to breathe a sigh of relief. As I listened to a lecture on her teachings, something profound struck me. Teresa was an advocate for a personal, heart-driven journey with Christ. The contemplative prayer experience that she outlined was one that an individual could create on their own only through the process of establishing a soul union with the Creator.

Per Saint Teresa, outside assistance wasn't necessary. The journey was the responsibility of each and every individual seeking God. It began in the hearts of every man and woman. Her beliefs aligned with the very message that had been churning in the pit of my stomach every day since I had committed to going down the path of a more advanced mentorship with my deceiver. It confirmed for me that my gut had been right all along. I didn't need him.

My personal faith journey would never be reliant on any other being. That was becoming clear. However, I still felt as though I needed further confirmation that my deceiver had intentionally been leading me astray. I wanted to definitively expose his path as one that was in conflict with my own. So I returned to my research of qigong. Something would not allow me to let it go. By early afternoon, I stumbled upon some research that gave me the answer I was seeking.

Qigong and tai chi are rooted in the idea of balanced energy, as energy is in all things created by God. This means a blending of hard and soft and good and evil. The "master" by the standards of these practices is not the one who is absolutely good but rather the one who has perfectly blended good and evil so that the end product is neither good nor evil. When you arrive at this state of blended energy, you essentially become God.

When I absorbed this message, it sent chills up my spine. I knew immediately that I needed to part ways with my deceiver. His motives and philosophies were coming into focus. This is why he had been encouraging me to accept the idea that "there is no evil." That "there will come a time when you will forgive and honor Lucifer." It was all rooted in a sick and twisted religion that sought to blend good and evil. He had been leading me down a path where he was going to invite me to create a union with a false god who had no definition of right and wrong. In that union, all morality would be lost, creating an earthly hell that would later extend deeper into the fiery pit for eternity.

I needed to slam the door closed on our relationship. I no longer had any doubts. It was time to resist. Without hesitancy, I turned away in the name of Jesus Christ. And the devil fled from me.

CHAPTER 23

THE FIRST TEMPTATION

HEDONISM

Then Jesus was led by the Spirit into the wilderness to be tempted by the devil. After fasting forty days and forty nights, he was hungry. The tempter came to him and said, "If you are the Son of God, tell these stones to become bread." Jesus answered, "It is written: 'Man shall not live on bread alone, but on every word that comes from the mouth of God.'" (Matthew 4:1–4)

WHEN THE SON OF GOD, JESUS CHRIST, WAS APPROACHED by the devil in the wilderness, he was confronted with three distinct temptations. In the span of eleven short verses captured in the Gospel of Matthew, we are offered a small glimpse of the nature of the deceit of the evil one. For a long time, I wondered why more depth was not shared. Then I met the devil myself, and the answer became clear.

A leopard never changes its spots. Now I understand that this notion seems counter to my depiction of the devil's chameleon-like nature. So allow me to explain. The evil one is indeed always adapting his visible message. But the foundational principles of his underlying schemes remain exactly what they were thousands of years ago. He has not changed his motives. He simply has allowed the sinful works of humanity to play into his hands as the world has crafted more and more means for disguising his work. The deception has become more intricate and harder to identify in modern times as we've grown conditioned to accept as a normal part of our daily lives the very things that are in opposition to the Will of God.

That's why we must "be alert and of sober mind" and go deeper to uncover the root of the threat. We must earnestly seek the underlying work of the evil one using the Word of God. Thankfully, the Gospel provides us with the three principle temptations behind the devil's schemes. God makes the root of the deception very clear. Our responsibility as children of God is prayerful discernment and resistance.

This first temptation experienced by Jesus at the hands of the devil was hedonism. Hedonism, by definition, is "the doctrine that pleasure or happiness is the sole or chief good in life." Hedonism means the avoidance of suffering. The foundational pursuit is well-being. By hedonistic standards, well-being is said to benefit from self-indulgence. Hedonists believe that we should focus on achieving the satisfaction of all of our sensual desires as that is essentially what creates the greatest good. Seeking pleasure takes precedence over seeking God.

Hedonism was the primary temptation that led me into the deception of the devil in our initial encounter. My life had been restored by the blood of Jesus. God had rescued me from the captivity of agoraphobia, giving my life new meaning and purpose. He allowed me to taste freedom once again. But it wasn't long until that freedom led me to a flesh-rooted desire to overindulge. I wanted more. So I took charge.

My focus shifted away from God and back onto my own pleasure-seeking desires. I began blindly pursuing the riches of the world to escape my own conviction. I had suffered long and hard, and I wanted things in my life that would make me feel good. So I abandoned the very real freedom of my rebirth in faith to seek highly perpetuated, false earthly freedoms. I didn't really want to own the responsibility of God's Will. I wanted only His healing measure. Then it was back to my desires. Sadly, I used God. I set Him aside. In doing so, I met His adversary, and soon after, I was led straight back to captivity.

By the time of my second encounter with the evil one, my intense appetite for pleasure-seeking freedom had diminished considerably. But my deceiver remained very hedonistic in nature. He did not attempt to hide that. His appetite for pleasure became most evident in the realm of sex. He was very open about his sexual encounters, and he seemed to consume women like chewing gum. He would use his power to seduce them and coerce them into bed having convinced them that all was pure and divinely inspired by the healing methods he was practicing. Then, as they lost their flavor or uncovered his motives, he would spit them out and move on to something new.

Any conversations that we had around the topic made me very uneasy. His contention was that my discomfort was rooted in the rigidity of my faith and the sexual phobias (obsessive-compulsive fears of getting a woman pregnant, for example) from my early adolescence. To him, I was a prude. He would poke and prod at me about that constantly, making light of sex and using language around it that really pushed my limits. He was often forceful in the manner that he did it. If I tried to divert the conversation, he would push through with the grotesque nature of his speech until I would finally oblige him to make him stop. Part of it was the agenda that he was attempting to have me adopt as my own, and another part was simply an open perversion that he could not possibly conceal.

The devil approached me about sex with the belief that I had a similar primitive, deep-rooted yearning for it that was consistent with most other males. In that, he was misled. I enjoyed sex with my wife, but I certainly was not controlled by it, not at this stage of my life. My faith had grounded me in that department many times. I didn't need sex, and I didn't sit around salivating for it throughout the day. Still, my deceiver seemed to believe that ultimately he would be able to trigger something within me to ignite that desire, and by doing so, he would then lead me away from God.

Sex became something that he frequently incorporated into metaphors about awakening a deeper spiritual transformation within me. This was something that really bothered me. Whenever I called him on it, he would arrogantly laugh it off and say things like, "Don't you think God has a sense of humor?" Because of course it was me, the stiff, conservative, dogmatic believer who had the issue.

According to him, God wanted us to enjoy the freedom of sexual pleasure, no matter how openly crude it may sound. The sanctity of sex by his standards was subjective in a sense so that if the actions were chosen and done with the pureness of intention, then that's what it was, even in the case of a one-night stand. There really were no boundaries.

That being said, my deceiver understood that I was married and I was fully committed to my wife. So he knew better than to push me to seek pleasure outside of our relationship. But he did not refrain from encouraging me to open up my wife sexually, essentially stating that as I grew more receptive, she would mirror me. In other words, if she was uncomfortable with something, it was simply a reflection that I was uncomfortable with something. If I wanted her to be more liberal in the bedroom, it had to begin with me.

I tried to share as little as possible with him about the intimacy in my relationship. There was, however, a day when I opened up to him about the closeness that I had experienced with my wife the night prior following a faith-led conversation we had with each other. In response, he said to me something along the lines of, "See? She's becoming more open because you are more openly receiving" what I am sharing with you. What he was stating was this: as you become more submissive to me, she'll become more submissive to you. He was staking claim to the intimacy in my marriage, assuming I wanted more of what I was receiving and asserting that in order to make that happen, I'd need to more deeply embrace his influence. In a sense, he was promising to give me more from my wife as I gave more of myself to him, thereby confirming that he had already assumed power over her as well.

Then there was the idea of the Kundalini awakening. Kundalini, of course, being the supposed coiled serpent, divine feminine energy found resting at the base of the spine per Hinduism. In the late days of my deception, my deceiver's infatuation with the Kundalini became increasingly visible. He began to attempt to introduce it to my marriage. The temptation: when she awakens the Kundalini, she is going to have a fierce sexual energy, so hold on to your hat. Go deeper with me, and through your own activation, you will learn how to activate her.

This sexual, pleasure-seeking awakening really seemed to be a critical element in the foundation of my deceiver's "religion." I remember at one point asking him what it would feel like when my soul had completed its journey to awakening, once I had ascended fully into my higher level of consciousness. He told me that it would be like "making love to God." A strange statement and one that he meant literally. That explained why he had often used such extremely perverse metaphors related to God. According to his deception, the most powerful sexual awakening that we could experience was tied directly to Him. That's where he wanted me to focus my energy and attention, on the temptation and away from the Truth.

Beyond the pleasure-seeking temptation, there was also the notion of avoiding suffering. It never much appealed to me because I understood that in order to carry the cross, I may need to walk a humbling road. In fact, I had recently come to the realization that I enjoyed the hardships that I encountered along my path. They always seemed to draw me closer to God. So I took delight in confronting pain because overcoming and transforming it fueled my being. I was beginning to feel that I may be led to a calling where

I would coach people through adversity. I recognized that I felt most alive and inspired when I was observing people scale walls and conquer personal demons.

I remember on one occasion sharing this idea with my deceiver. He quickly let me know he was in distinct opposition of it. He discouraged me by asking, "Do you really want to surround yourself with sick people?" He warned, "That will kill you." He advised me that if you're out seeking pain, that's all you are going to get in return. Then he shared with me his personal desire to seek to work with and heal people who were "ready to shoot their arrows into the light." He encouraged the same for me, belittling my past efforts to support those who were struggling. It seemed to me that he wanted what was dark within my community to remain that way.

Despite his best efforts to subdue the fire at my core, my passion for overcoming difficulty would not die. I remained active in my pursuit of pain. I believed I was at war each and every day with the devil, even though, ironically, I couldn't spot him right under my nose. I did know, however, that in order to be successful, I needed to challenge my mind and strengthen my faith. I had to continue training my hands for warfare in the spiritual realm. While my former teacher celebrated the pleasures of surrender, I continued to seek excess pain and fight. I knew that a battle for eternity was coming. And nothing had ever led me to believe that it was going to be a cakewalk for the children of God.

Of the three primary temptations presented to me by the devil, hedonism was probably the easiest for me to identify and resist in round two. I never felt moved to submit to a more committed relationship with him as a result of any hedonistic desire that he tried to awaken within me. Beyond the allure of pleasure, I certainly didn't believe that God desired us to live a pain-free existence, because pain was frequently the very thing that allowed me to grow closer to Him. Jesus had endured agonizing pain on the cross to overcome my sins. I was willing to suffer to serve His purpose in my life. After all that He had done for me, that was the least I could do for Him.

CHAPTER 24

THE SECOND TEMPTATION

EGOISM

Then the devil took him to the holy city and had him stand on the highest point of the temple. "If you are the Son of God," he said, "throw yourself down. For it is written 'He will command his angels concerning you, and they will lift you up in their hands, so that you will not strike your foot against a stone.'" Jesus answered him, "It is also written: 'Do not put the Lord your God to the test.'" (Matthew 4:5–7)

THE SECOND TEMPTATION SHARED IN THE GOSPEL IS egoism. Egoism by definition is the doctrine that individual self-interest is the actual motive of all conscious action. Could Jesus have sustained Himself following a leap from the top of the temple to prove to the devil that He was indeed the Son of God? Of course. Jesus Christ could walk on water. But He chose to deny the devil's temptation to prove His own personal might by expressing His reverence for His Father. Jesus understood that it was His Father's Will that would prevail. He didn't desire to challenge that with a prideful ego.

God's adversary is extraordinarily rich in ego. This was very evident to me by the time of our second meeting. It was a deeply revealing flaw of his that he could not hide. No matter how hard he tried to suppress it in my presence, it continued to show up. Even when he openly professed that he was moving away from his superiority complex and his anger toward those less spiritually evolved, his ego would command the stage as he began boasting about his latest transformation.

He was a chameleon who was sure of himself in any color. No matter the disguise, he LOVED it, and he was always proud to be the very best at wearing it. He made certain throughout our time with each other to ensure that I remained well below him in spiritual stature. How could I deny that? After all, I was speaking to an Ascended Master who embodied a fragment of the soul of Jesus.

Let's go back to the story of Lucifer for a moment. Remember that prior to the creation of humanity, Lucifer rebelled against God and was sent out of Heaven for eternity. In his obsession with his own strength and stature, he chose by his own free will to seek to rival God and create his own kingdom, thereby opening the door to sin. That's the very nature of the original sin that he introduced to Adam and Eve in the Garden of Eden as the serpent, or Satan, God's adversary.

In my time spent with the devil, one thing in particular became very clear. He had an unrelenting desire to assume the role of God, and he yearned to teach others how to realize that same power. Where I sought to be a representation of Christ in my thoughts, words, and deeds, my deceiver sought to actually obtain a godlike status to rival Christ. He believed that everything was essentially under his control. He taught that all matter was energy, and if you could master energy, you could achieve an elevated state of consciousness and place yourself on the level of a superior being.

My deceiver taught transcendental meditation to connect with other dimensions, and he claimed to have personal access to Ascended Masters such as Jesus Himself. This is why in my resistance to his notion that I should set aside the Word of God, he would often ask, "Would you rather have the teachings or the teacher?" and "Wouldn't it make sense to first meet the teacher and then revisit the teachings?" I'll admit, there were moments of weakness throughout my deception when that notion actually resonated with me. But who was to say that I was going to meet the real Jesus of Nazareth and not just some demon masquerading as Him?

A demon using His image to encourage me to do the will of evil.

You may be wondering, how could I ever think that someone could simply choose to give me access to Christ Himself? The answer is that I wanted to believe it. I had been waiting for my fight. I was now ready to stand and battle the dark forces of evil. I wanted to lead lost souls to salvation through Jesus Christ during the End Times. Sure, my deceiver's declarations were often extremely unusual and hard to absorb, but I slowly allowed myself to embrace them because I felt a strong connection to the purpose in all of it. I always believed there was something different about my spiritual journey that I had yet to uncover. Now, I thought, here it was.

My ego loved the idea that I was different. I felt truly inspired by the notion that we were a team of two called into a mission by a common God seeking to expose what was dark and be the Light of the world that would lead many more to salvation. I was so enamored by my calling that I began developing my own superiority complex as I dived deeper into my study of energy and spirituality. I started to view the church as being extremely dogmatic.

Interestingly, "dogma" was a word that had always driven me crazy when it was used by my former teacher to describe my own hesitancies. Now I was beginning to attach that same term to other Christians. I won't say that I was resentful of them, but I had this general belief that many believers were extraordinarily naive. I felt strongly that they were only scratching the surface of their faith because they weren't accessing the more mystical aspects of their relationship with God. Most certainly, they were not living their Truth. In fact, many were barely showing up.

I lost my compassion for individuals who began a faith journey only to meet resistance and turn back. That was a pretty self-centered move given the trials that I had experienced in my own story. I began to share in the resentment of my deceiver as my ego started to tell me that my path was superior to those who were unfit for the calling. I was taking risks in faith while they were floundering. I was strong and they were weak. They didn't deserve my time or energy. Spending my energy on them would only deplete my resources and limit my own capacity to serve those who were more worthy.

Sound familiar? If not, let me remind you. I was developing an infatuation with my own beauty and power, and I was revealing my desire to serve those deserving (as a god) through my own free will. I was aligning my steps with Lucifer while praising Jesus, and I didn't even recognize it.

Under the direction of my deceiver, I, too, became obsessed with energy. I started to believe as he taught that energy was in all things, and therefore, everything could be influenced and controlled by it. I became acutely aware of the energy in a room, and I could immediately sense the energy in people. Admittedly, this had always been a strength of mine. Hypersensitivity was one of my self-identified superpowers. That was something that my deceiver loved to exploit. Through his teachings, I began to feel that I could inspire an energetic shift by transforming or transmuting my own energy. I started trying to play a role in reworking every influence in my life.

When things didn't go according to my plan, I became quite overwhelmed. For example, when I felt as though my wife couldn't see the influence of negative energy present and make her own conscious shift as it started to lead to an imbalance in our home, I grew very frustrated and distant to her. My ego told me that she just didn't get it. She was not on my level. She was stuck in the natural plane fighting a battle with completely improper tools. My ego again declared that not everyone was cut out for the work that I was doing. Perhaps the bigger issue was that not everyone was ready to walk the fine line between accessing the depth of human capacity and seeking to become one's own god.

As I drew deeper into my ego, I began to pull away from God in the same manner that Lucifer did at the time of his defiant rebellion. I was being groomed to accept the notion that God's power was within me. That was an idea that didn't seem incompatible with my faith. I believe that most Christians would accept that as their Truth. But this is where the deception of the enemy gained its strength. This is where the lines became blurred.

The devil allowed me to believe that I was empowering the Spirit and living boldly in faith, but in reality, he was fueling my ego to embrace a greater reliance on my own godlike abilities. He knew I loved the idea that I embodied the electrical charge of the Holy Spirit. He recognized that I wanted the Spirit to direct my steps according to God's Will. So he used his deception to cause me to confuse the power of the Holy Spirit with my own egocentric intention to become one with God. I was seeking the Spirit to access my own supernatural, godlike power. Under the direction of Satan or the fallen angel, Lucifer, I slowly began my own rebellion.

The temptation of the ego was overwhelming. Ironically, the ego was the very thing that I believed I had been working to overcome and destroy. In reality, it was only gaining strength and becoming more of a threat to my soul's well-being. As I grew more infatuated with my own spiritual abilities, I felt moved to seek God more through meditation than I did through prayer. I believed that I could request permission to see and access things that I would have never been able to grasp in my less enlightened state, and so that's how I sought my answers. Not through reliance on God so much as through breathing and heart-centered intention. Although I did have visions, I am quite certain that many times, they were only a product of my own consciousness (what I wanted to see) and the demonic influence present (what Satan wanted me to see).

The practice that I was beginning to dabble in was quite dangerous. I was led to it directly by a temptation to access the capacity of God within me. I drifted from prayer. Even though I never set the Bible aside completely, I'd be lying if I said that I was actively seeking the Word as it was written. I wanted to hear it from the source and felt I had the power to go there and find it.

My deceiver fed the notion repeatedly that we were the trailblazers of this type of revolutionary spiritual transformation. I embraced that. So when he began advising me that I was only scratching the surface of my potential, I sensed that he was right, and my ego yearned for more. Of course, I was a little apprehensive. My gut often churned over the unknowns as my heart advised me to simply remain with Jesus in solitude. But my ego said, "Yes, please." The temptation to go deeper and fully step into oneness with God became extraordinarily hard to resist.

The devil was dangling the forbidden fruit in front of me and begging me to take a bite. I had no idea what would be revealed to me about myself, about the world and its people, or about God on the other side of my guided enlightenment. But I wanted to find out what had long been hidden from my view. I was gradually getting ready to accept the risks associated with taking that leap.

As we discussed what life would be like upon arrival at "ascension," I remember my deceiver once telling me that "you can never go back" to living as you once did. In my ignorance, I embraced that. The devil continuously schemed to make me feel as though I really didn't belong in and of this world. That resonated with me because it aligned with my faith. For Jesus once said to his disciples, "If the world hates you, keep in mind that it hated me first. If you belonged to the world, it would love you as its own. As it is, you do not belong to the world, but I have chosen you out of the world. That is why the world hates you" (John 15:18–19).

Satan's deception was the idea that an elevated state of consciousness would allow for ascension to a higher state of awareness within the very same world that I was already living. Further, that a "collective" ascension and awareness among other followers would somehow ultimately create a balance (or blend) between all things good and all things evil. This balance would then serve as harmony for all of humanity. No condemnation to Hell for evil. No promise of Heaven for the righteous and repentant. Per my deceiver, there could be no good or evil when God was in all things. And "everyone deserves salvation."

I was tired of the world in its current state. My deceiver felt empowered by that because it was in my detachment that I would be most prone to emboldening my own godlike abilities to change my reality and create the devil's depiction of eternal bliss. Rather than enduring hardship and carrying my cross to seek eternity in Heaven through the salvation offered by the blood of Jesus Christ, I would be led to seek salvation in the world through an elevated state of consciousness. Rather than overcoming the world through Jesus, I would instead make my bed in it for forever, guided by the boldness of my own ego. This was the story of Lucifer replaying itself in my own life.

Why does the devil tempt us with this egocentric idea that we can act as gods of consciousness and create our own Heaven on earth? Simple. Because he is stuck here for eternity. He hates God. He is at war with Him. And the best way for him to hurt God is to deceive His children and work to lead them astray. So what better deception to embody than the idea of a false Heaven of the world that promises no pain and no judgment, only perfect harmony?

Does anyone believe for a second that Heaven exists where both good and evil roam free? Think about that for a moment. Is that Heaven? No, that is Hell. That's exactly what the devil is tempting us with every single day. A worldly destiny. Hell on earth. He is running out of time. The Book of Revelation tells us that the destination where Satan is heading is far worse than any Hell that he could possibly create here on earth. I have no desire to take that ride with him. Do you?

CHAPTER 25

THE THIRD TEMPTATION

MATERIALISM

Again, the devil took him to a very high mountain and showed him all the kingdoms of the world and their splendor. "All this I will give you," he said, "if you will bow down and worship me." Jesus said to him, "Away from me, Satan! For it is written: 'Worship the Lord your God, and serve him only.'" Then the devil left him, and angels came and attended him. (Matthew 4:8–11)

THE THIRD AND FINAL TEMPTATION USED BY THE DEVIL against Jesus in the wilderness was materialism. Materialism is defined as a doctrine that the highest values or objectives lie in material well-being and in the furtherance of material progress. The devil was seeking to show Jesus all of the power and riches of the world in order to entice him to abandon the mission that He was sent to earth to fulfill as the Son of God.

Here again, this temptation is extraordinarily Luciferian in nature. The devil is the full embodiment of his own fall from grace. The temptations that he presents align with his own rebellion. In the earthly realm to which he was cast down, he was attempting to use the desires of the flesh to rob Jesus of the purpose that He was called to fulfill. That purpose was to defeat Satan—to overcome the world and the sins of humanity and to offer the promise of salvation to those who seek His truth. To offer eternity in Heaven to those who repent and believe.

When I began reflecting on the temptations of my deceiver, initially I had a more simplistic view of materialism in mind. I was viewing the temptation only for what it appeared to be to me on the surface. The promise of wealth and power. The praise of the people. The freedom from difficulty. The good life. Of course, all of those things are a part of it.

But the depth of this temptation is what is really revealing. It involves the devil's persuasion to abandon God for the sake of self. So it very much ties to the egoism that we visited in the second temptation. It's about silencing the Spirit to gratify the desires of the flesh. It's about pursuing the creation of a kingdom of Heaven on earth. Therefore, it's about coercing the Son of God to abort His Father's calling, which was to create a pathway to His Kingdom of Heaven through the forgiveness of sin. It's about steering the focus away from God so that the devil can continue to survive and thrive in the earthly realm to which he has been condemned.

Now let's begin by focusing on the easy stuff. In our initial meeting, the devil hooked me with the false promise of wealth. He used the allure of freedom through money to steer me away from God's calling for my life, and it worked. Shortly after my rebirth in Christ, I took the bait and fell into heavier financial burdens than I had ever experienced previously. For many years, I suffered the consequences of my rebellion. I was misled, but I was no victim. I chose my path against the Will of the Holy Spirit. I paid dearly for it.

Sadly, I didn't immediately learn from my mistakes. For years, I continued to seek to use my own strength to redeem myself, taking step after step in the wrong direction until I received my wake-up call and wholeheartedly turned back to God once again. It is true that old habits often die hard.

By the time I did finally arrive at a place of connectedness with my Creator once again, I was stronger and more mature. Money had ceased to be my primary motivation. The devil understood that I was no longer a slave to those desires. So in our second encounter, financial freedom wasn't a frontline temptation that he cared to employ. Since I had broken that stronghold in my life, he understood not to push me too hard in that respect, otherwise his identity may have been revealed.

When he began advocating for my commitment to advanced training, there were moments when I expressed concerns about accumulating debts. In response, he would often ask me, "Aren't you going to make a lot of money doing this healing?" to ease any worry that I may be experiencing with regard to my future ability to fulfill any payment obligations I had made to him. He always seemed happy to minimize the financial challenges of my past by telling me that I had accumulated debt simply because I anticipated it. He was making the argument that with a new intention, my future would be completely different. "Don't you have faith?" he would ask.

I remember when he shared with me a story about another individual whom he had been speaking to at around the same time. He was talking about the efforts that he had been making to convince that individual to align with him. He told me that he had asked the candidate very candidly, "Don't you want to make a million dollars?" Sheesh. That's a pretty rich promise. Not one that he ever made to me. This did reveal to me that my deceiver was still very open to tempting others through wealth. He just understood that money was no longer my venom. Therefore, he was more subtle in the way that he approached the topic around me. In fact, he would often act as though money wasn't a concern of his at all, stating that he was resigned to the fact that he wasn't supposed to become rich in his mission. As it related to any agreement that we made regarding my training, to him, "the alliance" was "more important than the money."

The alliance. There's an interesting pivot. Let's dive into that idea a little bit further as it relates to power. Remember that in the desert the devil asked Jesus to bow down and worship him, promising Him that if He chose to comply, he would give Him "all of the kingdoms of the world and their splendor." The devil, of course, has no power or authority in the realm of God. So he chose to scheme against the Son of God in presenting this temptation. He believed he could somehow gain access to heavenly power through a worldly alliance with Christ. If Jesus had made a deal with the devil, that would have meant that humanity would have remained captive to sin. The devil would have therefore retained all power over the world as the authority over the souls who were predestined for eternity in the heavenly realm because the Son of God chose to be submissive to him in the earthly plane. Of course, we all know that's not the way the story played out.

That being said, the devil hasn't stopped seeking alliances with the children of God. He promises power in his alliance because that's what he himself seeks from it. As I mentioned earlier, the devil is at war with God. The way that he does battle with Him is by attacking His children. He started with Adam and Eve and then he moved on to Jesus. Despite Jesus's victory over sin, the devil continues to seek believers all over the world. Particularly believers who threaten to disarm his ability to deceive his prey into relinquishing their rights to eternal salvation through the forgiveness of sin. To gain power, he needs an army of fallen believers. To assemble that army, he promises a share of his power.

My deceiver used the temptation of power in a variety of ways throughout our courtship. It was most influential when it was tied to the notion that I was chosen and predestined to fulfill a distinct role for God's Kingdom. Those ideas not only fueled my ego, but they also fulfilled a materialistic desire to be at the head of a movement that would lead people to eternal salvation. There was really no greater power that one could crave than to hold a role of authority as a guide for lost souls.

This role of authority tied directly into another aspect of the broader temptation, which is the adoration and praise of the people. As a leader in transformational spiritual healing, my deceiver taught that people would soon begin to seek me in the midst of turmoil. I would serve as the stillness in chaos. Like a beacon, my light would shine in the darkness. It would become a symbol of my miraculous awakening, and it would allow me to be revered for the state of my enlightenment. That reverence would give me great power in persuading others to follow the path to salvation that I (or perhaps we) had outlined for them.

The life promised by Satan at the time of my ultimate "ascension" in consciousness wasn't one that was simply rep-resentative of wealth, power, and adoration. It was also one of bliss. So I believe that this third and final temptation has ties to the very first as well. Within all of the devil's most twisted schemes against humanity, this may be one of the greatest. You see, the devil understands the groans of the flesh. He recognizes that humanity is prone to sin, to worldly pains, and to deception, because he is the author of all of those stories in our lives. He exposes us to adversity with evil intention to cause us to seek worldly remedies that promise peace and removal or distraction from the pain. Think about the root cause of all addiction.

It's a setup. The devil pokes and prods at us with the agony of the flesh, with earthly turmoil, and mental torment until one day we break. We decide that we can't take it anymore. We need to escape the pain and seek pleasure. That's when he hooks us in sin as he coerces us to stop trusting God and start seeking our own answers. When we begin making those types of decisions, we become extremely vulnerable to the temptation to turn away from the Word completely and instead seek our own supposed god within to heal ourselves on our own accord. Often in doing so, we open ourselves up to the influences of dark forces that promise a way to enlightenment and salvation beyond the Holy Spirit and the blood of Jesus.

Can you see a pattern beginning to unfold here? A surface-level analysis of each aspect of the materialism temptation reveals commonalities that outline the devil's grandest mission. That mission has always been to steer all believers, including the Son of God, Christ Jesus Himself, away from the Father. The same devil who once sought to deceive Christ in the wilderness is now seeking to deceive all of God's children by any means necessary into creating an alliance with him. When we align with the devil's temptations, God's mission and Will for our lives does not have the opportunity to unfold.

Imagine the fear and utter desperation of the evil one in the moment when Jesus began preparing to step into His ministry. He had to know that his days were numbered. By the time of this third and final temptation, Satan had reached his do-or-die moment. So he went deep into the bottom drawer and pulled out his last great invitation. In the strength of His Father, Jesus stood firm, slamming the proverbial door closed in the face of the devil and sending him running.

Jesus boldly accepted God's call for His life. He was not influenced in any way by the devil's materialistic advances, and He gave no thought to abandoning His own mission for the sake of gratifying any worldly desires. The story of Christ's resistance is incredibly inspiring. But we expect that sort of strength from the Son of God. He is the Almighty.

Jesus went into the wilderness to seek solitude with His Father and to confront His adversary. By the end of forty days of fasting, He knew His Father so intimately that He was able to immediately identify His antithesis when He was approached by him. He readied himself immediately with the armor of God, drawing on the sword of the Spirit, which is the Word of God to resist the devil's temptations.

When I was in the wilderness, I was seeking solitude and intimacy with my Creator as well. I wasn't, however, prepared for the approach and deception of my enemy. Thinking back now, it's pretty foolish that I would have expected God to make Himself known to me without any interference from His adversary. After all, I acknowledged the presence of dark forces in the world. I just didn't ever anticipate that I would come eye to eye with Satan. Even if I did, would I recognize him? If the devil didn't fit the depiction that I saw in Hollywood, how would I ever identify him?

This book is how. It took a pile of evidence, analysis, and deep reflection in God's Word to create the reveal. I wasn't nearly as equipped as Jesus was to deny the devil's temptations in the manner that He had done nearly two thousand years prior. I didn't know my Father in the intimate way that I had been called to receive Him. I believed I was strong in my faith, but in writing this story now, I can see quite clearly just how vulnerable I was during those seasons of my life. It's frightening to reflect on how close I was to following a path of deception that could have ultimately led me to sacrifice my mission and perhaps even my own soul to the hands of evil.

Although it encompasses many different things, the materialism temptation to me is rooted in a broad deception that disregards Jesus as the Savior. The devil was seeking to steer Jesus away from His Father's calling. A calling that would ultimately lead to His death on the cross, a sacrifice that would declare God's victory over sin. Remember, sin originated with the devil. Think back to Lucifer's rebellion and then later his conniving influence over Adam and Eve in the Garden of Eden. Satan introduced sin to humanity. God sent Jesus to overcome the work of Satan and offer humanity eternal salvation through the sacrifice of His one and only Son. So the only way that the devil's work could retain its power was through the disruption of Christ's mission. Satan had to deny the actions of Jesus as Savior.

Following the victory of Christ at Calvary, the devil was essentially rendered powerless. His only option moving forward was to act as though Christ's atonement had never happened. His goal has been to diminish the true Christ by deceptively steering believers away from the blood of the Lamb, depicting Jesus more simply as a prophet (or an Ascended Master, perhaps), thereby disregarding His sacrifice as the key to eternal salvation.

Salvation per my deceiver was available to all. I didn't deny this notion because I didn't feel that I was sitting in the seat of authority to do so. But I always believed that no matter the soul's avenue to God, Jesus would be waiting at the gates of Heaven, and entry would require an acknowledgment of Him as Lord and Savior. If sins remained open and unaddressed, then repentance for those sins existed as well. I stood firm in my belief that Jesus and His sacrifice was the key to eternity in Heaven.

As time passed in my relationship with my deceiver, I noticed that he was becoming more involved in working to establish a belief in me that there was a Jesus that I was missing. A more mystical presence whom I could access through transcendental meditation. An Ascended Master Jesus who could reveal the truth behind the teachings and share more of His wisdom than was ever captured in Scripture. This was the period when my deceiver began advising me to "set the Bible aside." He became bolder about announcing his own supposed ties to my Savior, eventually proclaiming, "I am Jesus!" because he "carried a fragment of His soul."

It was also at this stage when I began to notice his philosophy on the path to salvation beginning to emerge. He never shared it openly because he recognized that I hadn't yet been hooked. So there was still lots of deception in play. But despite his best efforts to conceal his true identity, I started to notice the shifting shadows in his teachings.

We had transitioned from the idea of collectively fighting the good fight to a definitive declaration that there was no evil in the world because God was in all things. My deceiver started to reveal beliefs that were reinforced by his endorsement of practices such as qigong. Then there was yoga and a more open embrace of the Hindu gods (which he had denounced previously) as he worked to educate me on the divine feminine energy (Kundalini). Bit by bit, I stockpiled the clues and worked to piece together the true nature of his religion.

My conclusion? As I mentioned in the previous chapter, my deceiver desired to build a coalition of followers who would abandon the Truth and act as his servants in creating what he described as Heaven on earth. In reality, his Heaven was Hell. Because it was his creation. It was a world where evil would run rampant without any consequence. There was not going to be any eternal salvation for humanity. That was all a lie because to him, there was no Jesus Christ the Savior. That was the key.

The devil desires condemnation through sin for all of humanity. That's why he introduced it in the garden. He wanted authority over the world that God had gifted to man and woman in the Book of Genesis. His mission on this earth has never been to save souls. It has always been to hold them captive. The only way he can accomplish his will is by steering the children of God away from the Truth and into alignment with his earthly temptations.

So he paints a pretty picture. Money, power, fame, bliss. All of the worldly pursuits that satisfy each and every desire of the flesh. He does this so that we lose ourselves in the idea that the things of the world carry greater weight than the eternal salvation of our souls. In a sense, the things of the world become the gods that we worship. Ultimately, by submitting to his false religion, we too aspire to become gods so that we never have to answer to anyone for right or wrong. The devil's corrupt notion of salvation is built on the harmonic blend of good and evil and not on the repentance of sin and the merciful blood of Jesus Christ.

This falling away of humanity from God that we are witnessing today is Lucifer's self-seeking story repeating itself in modern times. It was Lucifer, now regarded as Satan, who was the author of the original sin. He is the mastermind behind the great temptations that continue to seek to undermine God's greatest gift to his beloved children to this very day. That gift is the blood of the Lamb. The redeeming sacrifice of God's one and only Son, Jesus Christ. The greatest act of love ever committed.

CHAPTER 26

CALLED OUT OF THE WILDERNESS

Nevertheless, each person should live as a believer in whatever situation the Lord has assigned to them, just as God has called them. This is the rule I lay down in all the churches. (1 Corinthians 7:17)

IT WAS 2:39 A.M. JUST A COUPLE OF DAYS AFTER MY resistance of the evil one. Something had stirred me awake about an hour prior, and I was lying in bed reflecting on all my experiences with my deceiver. I kept asking myself, what does this all mean? What will it reveal to me about the next step in the evolution of my spiritual journey? Then I felt God speak.

My wife was asleep, so I wasn't going to wake her, but I knew I needed to share with her what I believed in that moment

I was being led by God to do. So I sent a text message to her phone, which read, "I have been thinking more deeply into this whole great deception that I went through, and it's truly wicked. Putting the pieces of the puzzle together, it's making more sense why it unfolded in the way that it did. I need to write this story adding my research and clarity as it arrives. It's going to be pretty wild." I didn't know it at the time, but I recognized soon after that this message would serve as my declaration of war with the devil.

When I drifted back to sleep in the early morning hours, I was led to a dream. It was the most powerful dream that I had ever experienced in my entire life. Yet, when I woke to the sound of my alarm at 5:30 a.m., it was no longer immediately front of mind. The dream was buried in my subconscious. So I went about my normal routine, traveling over to the nearby park where I spent my time in solitude with God running at dawn.

On this particular morning, I felt a nudge to do something a little bit different, to break off the trails that I had taken through the wilderness and head over to the center of the community where many of the local businesses were housed. I felt as though I was hearing God say, "It's time. Take the message to them." So I adjusted my path, and I began running laps around the village square. It was about a half-mile loop. I believe that I was midway through my second lap when my dream from a few hours earlier hit me, and I felt the Holy Spirit flood my being like a wave of Truth. I knew that I was about to uncover a breakthrough. So as I continued running, I began to peel back the layers.

In the dream, I was with my wife. We were stepping through a door and into a home, which seemed to be within an apartment building because it had an inside entry, and we were on a higher floor. You could say that it felt a bit like a hotel, but inside the front door, it very much resembled what you may expect to see in a typical single-story apartment home.

Just inside the door, there was a kitchen area that had been completely destroyed. Things were scattered everywhere. On the ceiling in the kitchen was a fluorescent light, and that was the only light source illuminated within the home. As I stepped delicately through the rampant chaos that appeared to be the work of paranormal, poltergeist-like activity, I felt drawn to the bedroom. I made my way back down a short hallway to the master bedroom door, which had been drawn closed.

When I clutched the handle, I remember attempting to pull the door open toward me, and there was this incredibly powerful, invisible force fighting in resistance to keep the room sealed closed. I pulled with all of my might, and eventually I was able to gain entry.

What I found beyond the threshold was terrifying. It was

dark, and there was a fierce wind circulating. Yet, there was no evidence of open windows. Furniture was flying all over the room. The energy was absolutely sinister. I knew that the invisible enemy was Satan and his legion of demons. So I began resisting, calling on the Word of God and denying the evil spirits in the name of Jesus Christ. It was spiritual warfare. My actions resembled something that you might witness in an exorcism.

The thing that really stuck with me was the power of the enemy's resistance. As I began to attempt to form the words in my mouth to cast out of the home the wicked forces at play, the devil made every desperate move possible to silence me. It felt as if I was trying to scream while I was being choked. Imagine summoning every ounce of your strength to draw all of your power to your throat and bring the words to your lips and still you couldn't speak. The devil seemed fully aware of the fate that he would suffer when confronted with the Word of God. He wanted absolutely no part of me bringing it to him.

In the dream, I remember having this resiliency that was not going to allow for a retreat. I was going to push through the evil resistance and speak the Word because I understood that this was the work that I was called to do. I had no fear, only confidence. I was led by a boldness that only God could command. I reached deep inside, calling on the power of the Spirit to bring the words out of my mouth. What began as an insistent groan soon turned into a passionate battle cry in the name of Jesus Christ. It wasn't long before the words started flowing out of my mouth like a flood. I felt the energy in the room begin to shift.

The wind stopped, the furniture stood still, and a state of calm returned to the bedroom and the entire home. Satan and his demonic forces had surrendered to the Word and to the Holy Spirit. I was not shocked by that in the slightest. I knew the power of the armor of God. It seemed that I had done this work before.

Having handled the demons inside of the apartment, my wife and I then exited the home together and made our way down a hallway and to an elevator. We entered and set the dial for the lobby, and when the doors opened, we met my father there. Soon we were surrounded by a number of other figures from my past.

We were all having a conversation related to tickets. It seemed that we were planning to attend an event together. The figures from my past were waiting for me to distribute their tickets for admission. I remember that my father already had his reservation in hand, so I knew that his seat was secure. Then there was my wife, who I would, of course, be bringing with me. Beyond that, I recognized that I didn't have enough seats for everyone. I was really concerned. What would I do?

A couple of old friends from my past, neither of whom have I spoken to in many years, approached me and said they had found a couple of tickets through someone who was selling them nearby. I cautioned them, "How do you know that those are legitimate? Where did you get them? There are lots of fakes, and you don't want to get caught up in that. You're not going to get what you are anticipating. Be careful."

Then I remember that my father looked at me with a sense of urgency in his eyes. He was ready to go. I understood that he always liked to be early. I checked the time and it was 3:50 p.m. Our event was at 4:00 p.m. We would still make it on time, but my arrival wasn't going to be well in advance because I was feeling called to revisit the apartment upstairs and check on the activity.

When I returned there with my wife, the kitchen was calm and in good order, but as I walked toward the short hallway and pulled on the door handle of the bedroom, I noticed that the demonic resistance was back once again. This time, however, it was considerably weaker than it had been during my initial encounter. It could no longer cling to my throat and prevent the words of Truth from forming on my lips. In its weakened state, I disposed of it quickly, again drawing on the Word of God as my artillery.

Moments later, I woke up.

Sadly, I never was able to witness the event that we were preparing to attend. The setup in the lobby felt a lot like a college football Saturday, but I sensed in my reflection that we were headed to witness something far greater. The look in my father's eyes had confirmed the magnitude of the event. He was holding his ticket in his hand as if everything that he had ever desired depended on it. My father loved football. He loved being early for a kickoff. But this wasn't just another football game. This was THE event that he had waited for his entire life. There was absolutely no chance that he was going to miss it. I wondered, were we preparing to witness the second coming of Christ?

As I continued my laps around the village circle, I kept reflecting more deeply into the meaning of my dream, and I began connecting the dots and drawing conclusions. The battle with the demonic forces in the apartment, the spiritual warfare—this was most certainly one aspect of my calling being revealed. The devil would try to silence me in my mission, but the Holy Spirit and God's Will would ultimately prevail. I would fight the darkness until the very moment that Jesus Christ returned to call us home. My wife would be there with me. I would never leave her behind on my journey. She may not ever seek the fight in the same manner as me, but she would remain a loyal, steady presence and would always support me and follow the faith wherever it led us in our marriage.

My father's presence was so telling. When I was trapped in

the darkest season of my life, my father was the individual who reintroduced me to the Word of God. He purchased a Bible for me and opened the door to devotional studies that allowed me to create a deeper relationship with my Creator. That relationship then led me to a faith-guided healing path that was nothing short of miraculous in nature. I owe so much to him for what I ultimately gained from the Word of God. His faith was the Light that I needed to find the courage to begin navigating the darkness in my own spiritual journey.

Then there was this idea of tickets. Tickets for the event that we were all planning to attend. If that event was as I had surmised the second coming of Jesus Christ, then it would only stand to reason that the ticket would be needed to gain entry into God's Kingdom in Heaven. That's why perhaps these seats were so deeply coveted.

My father's ticket was a given. He was ready. He was watching the time, eagerly anticipating the event, and he planned to be early. I would be planning to attend as well. Naturally, I would be bringing my wife along with me. But my challenge was that I didn't have enough tickets to distribute to all of the figures from my past who desired to go with us.

What was I going to do? I couldn't allow them to be deceived by scalpers who would sell them a useless ticket. But I didn't have a means to let them gain entry on my own accord. I recognized that I was not the source. That was clear. I could not print my own tickets. I could, however, help to guide them to the one true source. Aha, that was it. Confirmation of the second aspect of my calling. It is to guide those lost and seeking to the Truth in Jesus Christ so that they can achieve their eternal salvation and enter God's Kingdom in glory on the day of His triumphant return.

That morning following my run, I returned home with a fire burning in my belly to get to work fulfilling God's Will. I had declared war with the devil and I was moving to the front line. I would no longer allow him to silence the Spirit that had begun overflowing within me. For the rest of my life, I would rely on the strength of God. Together, we would persevere in the face of any resistance that the evil one presented. I would no longer run from the enemy. I would challenge and destroy him armed with the Word, pressing forward in the Truth until the very moment when Jesus appeared in the sky to call me home. I would live my testimony openly so I might inspire others to develop a relationship with Christ and gain their own eternal salvation through His blood.

In May of 2012, I wrote a thirty-two-page manuscript proposal to secure a deal with a publisher and share my story in print. Once my publishing agreement was in place and it was time to begin writing, I quickly allowed the influence of my flesh to lead me back into the hands of the devil. I made the decision to set the project aside, offering every possible excuse that you could imagine to justify my retreat.

Abandoning my publishing deal was one of the greatest regrets of my life. But I always had this feeling that the project may be resurrected at some point. I had begun to contemplate writing once again, but I understood that with all of the time that had passed since my initial proposal, whatever I developed would need to be a new vision altogether. I was not the same person I was back then. The depth of my experience had accelerated in recent years. I had a much more mature perspective to share.

But I needed more than just a story in order to get started. I needed a calling. A story would make a great contribution to a blog, but only a calling would allow me to overcome the fearful resistance that would accompany the magnitude of a book project. Now I had it. I knew with great certainty that I had been given my calling. A calling of a significance far superior to fear.

There was no turning back now. I recognized in my heart that it was time to start writing. So without hesitation, on that very same day, I opened a Word document and began developing the first chapter of *The Devil and the Children of God at the End of the World.*

CHAPTER 27

THE LION AND THE LAMB

Be alert and of sober mind. Your enemy the devil prowls around
like a roaring lion looking for someone to devour. (1 Peter 5:8)

THINK ABOUT THIS PIECE OF SCRIPTURE FOR A MOMENT.
Lions roar to show their prowess and to stake claim to their
territory and their pride. The apostle Peter is identifying
Satan, the adversary of God as the lion. Much like the lion
who seeks to reign over the animal kingdom, Satan is boldly
seeking to lay claim to the world and the children of God
who live in the world.

Now, in the animal kingdom, we know that lions sleep an
average of twenty hours per day. But the lion that Peter
describes is not a lion at rest. This is a lion that is active. He
is "prowling" and aggressively seeking his prey. In contrast

to the lions that we see in the natural world, the lion of the spiritual realm (Satan) is always on the move. His appetite never diminishes. He is always hunting and aggressively seeking to expand his dominion in the earth. You could say that he is relentless. That's why we must be alert and of sober mind. The devil doesn't take days off and he doesn't break for rest. He may arrive at any time. Like the lion of the jungle, he will frequently choose the very moment that we let our guards down to pounce. So we must be ready.

But what does "ready" mean in the spiritual world? How do we prepare for the approach of a lion that we cannot see? A lion that prowls and roars in silence. A lion with a growing pride disguised by the human form. His teachings hidden within the vessels of the captive souls that he has deceived and marked as his own. Vessels that often far too easily blend into the communities in which we live. How do we escape being devoured by the devil when he so closely mirrors everything that we have come to know and accept as ordinary?

We must first begin to detach ourselves from the corrupt nature of the world around us. The Bible tells us in 1 John 2:16–17 that "everything in the world—the lust of the flesh, the lust of the eyes, and the pride of life—comes not from the Father but from the world." That "the world and its desires pass away, but whoever does the will of God lives forever." The world is at odds with God. So if we allow ourselves to be influenced by the world, we cannot remain in God. The moment we begin a love affair with the world and the desires of our flesh, we open the door to the devil's will: a will that is rooted in a fate where death is a certainty. But if we instead choose to remain in God in the midst of any worldly opposition that we encounter, then our eternity will be sealed in Heaven with our Creator.

Perhaps the question needs to be asked, "Are we living for today, or are we living for eternity?" If we are living for today, we are deeply vulnerable. We are like the sleeping gazelle lying in the open of a sunlit and treeless safari. The devil and his pride are quickly approaching, salivating, and eagerly getting ready to pounce. If you were watching this scenario unfold in a wildlife documentary on your television, this is the very moment when you would yell, "Wake up!" Because on the screen, you can recognize the threat. I'm here to tell you that God is always watching your story reveal itself before His eyes. Even though the enemy may remain hidden from your view, God is never unaware of the presence of evil.

If you are sleeping in the false security of the world, He may be begging and pleading with you in this moment to "wake up!" After all, you are His child. The Father does not wish to see His child be devoured by a roaring lion. God desires you. He is seeking your soul for eternity. So awaken and resist.

Awakening means that you take the war for your soul seriously. Every single day, you must rise and "put on the full armor of God" as described in Ephesians chapter 6 "so that you can take your stand against the devil's schemes."

In the midst of my greatest temptation, I began to understand just how very critical it was that I purify myself in the blood of Christ every single day. When I began spending time with my Creator at dawn, I would repeatedly make an effort to ensure that I concluded my run at the "sacred place" that I had identified when my spiritual transformation began to take root. That place was the little creek hidden under the canopy of trees adjacent to the path where I spent time alone with God. Every day, I would approach the water, pray and bless it, and then perform a makeshift baptism ritual on myself. In that ritual, I would feel God's love, mercy, and grace wash over me. It was a deeply rejuvenating experience each and every time. On the days when I wasn't able to get there, I noticed that I didn't feel nearly as clear or as grounded.

In that sacred space, I witnessed countless miracles. It was there that I prayed earnestly seeking to reveal the true nature of my deceiver. It was there that I began to feel the churning in my stomach as the Truth worked to make itself known. It was there that I prayed following my resistance of the devil for God to draw anything dark and decaying out of me as I sensed a tormenting evil presence circling. That's where I felt that sinister presence leave my body as I nearly blacked out and fell to the ground as it was disposed of by the Lord.

With the help of God, I uncovered the prowling lion just moments before he was ready to devour me. What saved me was the divine recognition that every single day, I needed to wash myself clean in the Spirit of the Lord. Perhaps a daily baptism isn't necessary for everyone, but we must all make a committed effort to seek Him through prayer and the Word daily. Because every new morning without fail, the spider weaves its web. In order to avoid that web of deception and captivity, we need to remain committed to waking up "sober and alert" with a heart centered on seeking God. The devil is always in relentless pursuit, eagerly awaiting a guard that we've let down, like a lion yearning to pounce.

My savior is the Lamb of God. When we think of a lamb, we think of childlike vulnerability. After all, a lamb is a baby sheep. Isn't it remarkable that God chose a lamb to overcome the "roaring lion" of the world? As we approach the End Times, the children of God need to keep their eyes focused on the Lamb and not the lion. John speaks of the Lamb twenty-eight times in the Book of Revelation alone. We must remember that Jesus won the battle at Calvary as the slain Lamb of God. So when He returns, He will simply be seeking to claim what is rightfully His, the children of God whom He will welcome into the Kingdom of Heaven.

The devil cannot rob you of the victory of the Lamb. As believers, it is ours for the taking. If we repent of our sins and invite Jesus Christ to come into our hearts and direct our steps according to His Will, the promise is there always. No matter the appetite of the lion, the devil cannot change the outcome. God loves His children. He loves them so much that He sent His only Son as a sacrifice for our sins. He overcame the world and all of the forces of evil so that we could be set free. That's the Father.

Like a lamb, we must enter God's Kingdom in childlike obedience to the Will of our Father. In preparation, we must seek the vulnerability of a life rooted in faith in a world that is in opposition to the Truth. By the standards of this age, this is no small task. It requires great courage. But it is the only way. We cannot receive the promise without living our faith in the Father with the pure vulnerability of that of His child.

In order to receive faith as a child, we must deny the influences of the invisible enemy. How do you avoid stumbling in a room filled with darkness? You turn on a light (or the Spirit and the Word of God) and awaken to reveal the nature of the obstacles along your path. Then you begin cleaning up the clutter. So the next time when you begin stepping through the darkness, you can rest assured that your feet will land on secure ground.

When I was young, I was completely unaware of the threatening presence of my adversary. Perhaps that was by design. Choosing to reveal the influence of the evil one to your children is a tough call. Whether you decide to have the conversation or to avoid it, the fact of the matter is that he is present. He is active. So it's critical that your children know how to illuminate the path. This is the legacy that I seek to leave behind for both my son and my daughter through the work in my mission.

Leading by example is so critical for parents. If as a child we witness our family in prayer and in the Word, if we hear them talk about and praise God, and if we observe them actively turning away from the influences of the world, then we as children will likely follow their example. That's obedience. In other words, if we want them to know the Father, then we better embody everything that He is ourselves.

God does not wish to see any of His children left behind. I am testament to that as a son who was lost and later found on more than one occasion. The Father is patient. He is filled with compassion beyond our natural ability to comprehend. There are children who grow up without any knowledge of Jesus Christ because they were raised in homes where He was not welcome. That does not mean that God loves those children any less. Every child is a reflection of His perfect creation. He desires that each and every one of us come home to Him. So I believe that He will always make a path.

My prayer is that this book for some of you may serve as that path. I am here to remind you that YOU are a child of God.

And I'd like to invite you home today. If the roaring lion has led you into the darkness to devour you, resist and stand firm in the Truth. Repent and draw near to God. Fulfill His perfect will for your life. Be saved by the blood of the Lamb. Set yourself free. This is the Father's desire. You were chosen.

Study the Word of God. Remember that it is your sword. Empower the Holy Spirit. This is how the Father will cover you in His loving protection. It's that simple. It has always been. Victory is His. It's our mission as believers to boldly go out and claim it.

On the day of the devil's great temptation in your life, I pray that my testimony will help you to expose the work of the evil one and bring all that is dark to the one true Light, the Light of God.

Never forget:

> No temptation has overtaken you except what is common to mankind. And God is faithful; he will not let you be tempted beyond what you can bear. But when you are tempted, he will also provide a way out so that you can endure it. (1 Corinthians 10:13)

The return of Jesus Christ is nearing. So fight the good fight. Keep watch for the white horse, whose rider is called Faithful and True. The King of Kings and Lord of Lords. The Alpha and the Omega, the First and the Last, the Beginning and the End. The triumphant Lamb of God! Hallelujah!

ABOUT THE AUTHOR

MATTHEW DEIBLER is the founder of The Lamp on the Stand Motivational Ministry, a leading content development, leadership, and coaching firm committed to inspiring faith-led transformation. He is an outspoken mental health advocate with nearly a decade of powerful influence in the mental health community, where he has boldly shared the riveting story of his own spiritual rebirth and restoration from the depths of panic-ridden agoraphobia, obsessive-compulsive disorder, and addiction. Matthew is the founder of The Outlet, a natural dialogue mental health community that recharges its members with positivity, faith, and gratitude. He is dedicated to living his purpose as a messenger of hope and an ambassador of Truth, twenty-four hours at a time with a mindset focused on eternity. Matthew is a 2005 graduate of the University of North Carolina at Chapel

Hill. He is a devoted husband and the proud father of two beautiful children. To learn more about his mission or to contact Matthew directly, please visit lamponthestand.com.

Made in the USA
Columbia, SC
09 March 2021